STEP-BY-STEP GARDEN PROJECTS

Martin Walters

Gardens for Wildlife

Practical advice on how to attract
wildlife to your garden

AURA BOOKS

Aura Garden Guides

Gardens for Wildlife

Martin Walters

Copyright © 2007 Baker & Taylor Limited,
Bicester, England

This edition produced by:
Transedition Limited for:
Baker & Taylor (UK) Ltd,
Bicester, England

Typesetting:
Asgard Publishing Services, Leeds

Picture credits
All pictures from Natural Visions. All pictures by
Heather Angel except for those by: M & J Bloom-
field 52, 64; Richard Ford 34, 55; David Harrison
46; David Hector 50; Chris Newman 47; Paul
Ormerod 44; Brian Rogers 32, 66t; Paul Sawer
26b, 39, 42, 45, 51, 58, 74; Jason Venus 48

All drawings by Michael C. Wood

10 9 8 7 6 5 4 3

Printed in Dubai

ISBN 978 1905765 041

Martin Walters is a writer, editor and
naturalist. A keen watcher of garden
wildlife, he also has a special interest in
plants, habitats and conservation.

Growing up in a wildlife-friendly botanic
garden inspired him from an early age with
an interest in the use made by wildlife of
garden plants, both native and exotic.

Martin has published regularly. His books
include field guides to birds and flowers,
and many nature reference works.

CONTENTS

Introduction

This book is complementary to the previous book in this series: *Gardens for Birds*. Although birds are the most visible and popular group of animals we see in our gardens, wildlife covers a far wider range of animals and plants, all of which are fascinating and attractive in their own right, and without which there would be no birds in your garden.

Gardens for Wildlife is intended to be an introductory guide to making your garden as wildlife-friendly as possible. Although it includes notes on the commonest species visiting gardens, it does not provide an identification guide. There are many other books available for identifying garden wildlife, and this book can be used in conjunction with established guides to our native flowers, mammals, birds, reptiles, insects, and other animal and plant life (see page 79).

In the first part of the book we explain the basic steps involved in planning a wildlife garden – one that is attractive to many forms of wild animals (and plants) – and we show you how to create a variety of habitats within the space available, suggesting suitable species of trees, shrubs and other plants, both native and exotic. We also explain the importance of having a wildlife pond, and how to provide habitats for invertebrates as well as for the larger and more prominent groups such as mammals and birds.

In the section that follows we look at wildlife from the viewpoint of the impact which some species have on gardens, highlighting those that are definitely beneficial, and suggesting some ways of deterring undesirable species.

Even a relatively formal suburban garden can be rendered more wildlife-friendly by the use of bird baths, a pond and a varied planting, with ferns for cover and flowers for insects.

The main part of the book consists of a handy directory of garden wildlife, concentrating on those animals most likely to be seen in our gardens. The section on birds includes only the commonest species, and the companion book *Gardens for Birds* is recommended for more detailed coverage. Each species or group of species has a brief description followed by information on distribution, status and habitat, and food preferences where relevant.

The final section is a summary of useful information for the wildlife gardener, listing relevant organisations and suggesting some further reading.

Changing fashions in garden design

Fashions in gardening have changed and evolved over the centuries, and also in recent years. These days many gardeners have come to understand the benefits of creating a garden that is both a beautiful inspiration and a safe haven for wildlife. As any visitor to garden shows will appreciate, the range of garden types is wide, but most such shows now tend to include at least one wild garden – and 'wild' need not mean untended and scruffy. We can indeed create a garden that is both wildlife-friendly and aesthetically pleasing.

Wildlife-friendly gardening, then, is becoming increasingly popular, and the trend is now away from manicured, sterile lawns, flanked by clipped hedges and shrubs, to gardens planned not just for the plants, but also for the benefit of wildlife. This is healthier all round, for it means using fewer chemicals such as pesticides and weedkillers – after all, in a balanced, ecological garden, many pests are destroyed by their own predators, because the natural food-chains of predator and prey can be maintained. This doesn't rule out the occasional use of artificial inputs, but staying as close to nature as possible is certainly the best route for attracting wildlife to your garden.

Many people nowadays are successfully re-creating 'natural' habitats in their own gardens. Lawns, for example – or at least sections of them – can be turned into flower-rich meadows by allowing the grasses and herbs to grow tall, then cutting a hay crop once or twice a year. This gives the small mammals and birds a range of seeds and insects to eat, and also attracts butterflies and other useful invertebrates.

Attracting wildlife to your garden

Gardening with and for wildlife is now increasingly popular, as we begin to understand the benefits to our own health, and that of our environment, that can result from following more natural guidelines.

Interest in wildlife has never been higher, as is testified by the growing membership of organisations such as the Wildlife Trusts, the Royal

If you have sufficient space, it is good practice to allow some of the grass to mature and grow tall. Eventually wild flowers will grow up amongst the grasses and the wildlife in your garden will certainly be enriched – the more so if you are fortunate enough to have adjacent trees and shrubs, as here.

Society for the Protection of Birds (RSPB) and Buglife (the Invertebrate Conservation Trust). Britain has a diverse range of habitats and reserves, excellent access to the countryside, and a long history of nature conservation.

Yet natural habitats and traditional, low-intensity farming are continuing to disappear, as more and more land is required for housing and road building. This trend has been slightly reversed with grants encouraging farmers to maintain wild sites on their land. Nevertheless, our wildlife remains under threat. For this reason, the green reservoirs represented by the patchwork of parks and gardens in villages, towns and cities are ever more important for our wildlife. Gardens today are arguably some of the richest of all the habitats available to wildlife. Thus the single most important contribution we can all make to enhance the biodiversity of our country lies right before us, in our very own gardens and backyards.

There are also specific things you can do to attract wildlife, such as:

- providing food for the various species, particularly at times when natural food sources are scarce

- putting up nest boxes or planting cover to encourage the use of more natural sites for shelter and nesting.

For birds in particular there are many food suppliers and a surprisingly large range of nest boxes available, not just for robins and tits, but also for 'fussier' birds such as owls, house martins and even swifts. It is a great pleasure to watch birds taking food to the nest – gardens are productive breeding sites for a number of birds, many of which have invaded gardens from their original woodland or hedgerow habitats. Many of these suppliers also offer

This well-planted border is full of late-summer flowers, including Agapanthus, Sedum spectabile *and* Artemisia ludovicorum.

other wildlife equipment such as hedgehog shelters, bat boxes and even shelters and nesting sites for insects such as hoverflies and bees.

While birds are undoubtedly the most prominent group in the wildlife garden, there is a also a wealth of other groups – notably mammals, many types of insects and other invertebrates – and these are just as important in the ecology of the balanced 'natural' wildlife garden. Indeed, without these other creatures, we would have far fewer birds. Gardening for insects and less prominent wildlife will also guarantee a rich birdlife.

Hollyhocks (Alcea rosea) *are particularly attractive to bees.*

For the true wildlife gardener a number of techniques can be used. One way is to go with the flow in your own garden: find out, by trial and error, which plants do best and which suffer from predators and pests, and then increase the former and allow the latter to diminish. In a snail-rich garden, for example, plants such as sweet peas and morning glories are hard to protect from damage, while busy lizzies, diascias and pelargoniums, as well as aromatic species like mint, sage and lavender, survive relatively unscathed.

Another method is to alter the nature of the soil surface around plants, by using gravel or sand to deter snails, or containers to create barriers.

If we encourage native wild flowers and other plants to grow in our gardens, we are not only providing habitats for native animals, but the plants themselves are more likely to survive well, having evolved alongside the native animals that attack them. On the other hand, introduced species – both animals and plants – may be more of a problem, and some of these have become serious pests.

Another form of natural pest control comes from the wildlife itself. The more diverse the wildlife you can attract to your garden, the less likely will any

 Key points

The key points to bear in mind for increasing the numbers and range of wildlife in your garden are:

- Create diverse habitats.
- Avoid or minimise the use of chemicals.
- Offer a choice of healthy food.
- Provide attractive sites for nesting, including nest boxes.

particular pest species be able to take a hold – thus song thrushes eat snails, while ladybirds and lacewings consume aphids, certain centipedes prey on slugs, and many wasps and their relatives feed on a range of small insects, helping to reduce the numbers of many of those we consider undesirable.

There is a philosophical point to be made here as well. One gardener's weed can be another's delight, and just as a weed may be defined as a plant regarded as being in the wrong place, so animal 'pests' are themselves part of wildlife and are (to many people) interesting in their own right. That very snail or slug that has just munched through your lettuce may well end up helping to sustain the local song thrush whose morning song is such a delight!

Natural pest control

Wildlife and chemicals do not go well together, so if wildlife is to flourish, minimising or eliminating the use of weed-killers and other poisons in the garden is essential. Some knowledge of the biology of garden wildlife allows us to work with nature to harness the effects of natural predators in controlling various troublesome pests.

That said, there are a (surprisingly small) number of pest species that can have severe effects on garden plants in particular, so the question immediately arises: how can these pests be controlled without the use of chemical sprays and pellets?

Features of a small wildlife-friendly garden

1 *A wildlife tower in front of a buddleia (a magnet for butterflies)*

2 *Tall trees (if space allows) where a squirrel feeder, roosting pouch or bat box or may be placed*

3 *Fruiting trees and shrubs provide food for insects and birds*

4 *Dense hedges give good cover*

5 *Well-stocked borders with plenty of nectar-rich flowers*

6 *A bird feeder*

7 *Fences covered in climbers such as honeysuckle*

8 *A small wild meadow*

9 *A pond with a small boggy area behind*

10 *A pile of rotting logs*

11 *Water butts*

Features of a larger wildlife-friendly garden

1 Borders stocked with food plants for birds and insects

2 A large pond with aquatic and marginal plants

3 Adjoining boggy area

4 A shady border with ferns – damp shelter for amphibians

5 Dry, sunny borders with rocks where creatures can bask

6 Areas of grass with different cutting regimes

7 A taller meadow

8 Fruit trees, with some fruit left for birds and other animals

9 Large shrubs provide dense cover for a hedgehog box

10 A group of native trees with nest boxes and bat boxes

11 Dense hedges provide cover

12 A quiet, sunny corner with nettle beds and compost bins

Planning the wildlife garden

Why create a wildlife garden?

Creating a wildlife garden is important for conservation. Natural or semi-natural wildlife sites such as ancient woods, heaths and flower-rich meadows are under increasing threat. For example, 90% of our flower meadows have been lost in recent times, and 70% of British butterflies have declined in the last 20 years.

Britain has an estimated 15 million gardens, which together preserve 270,000 hectares of land – an area larger than all the UK's National Nature Reserves combined. In this situation, the importance of individual gardens for wildlife cannot be overestimated.

Although gardens may often be small, they frequently link up to form wildlife corridors along which animals, especially birds, move freely from one garden to another.

How to create a nature-friendly garden

One of the most important principles to follow when designing a nature-friendly garden is to strive for as much variety as possible, unless of course space is extremely limited. In general, the greater the diversity of habitat you can

provide, the greater will be the range of species your garden will attract. Thus an ideal wildlife garden might have:

- one or more tall trees
- a hedge
- well-stocked borders
- an area of lawn, part of which would be a flower meadow
- a nettle patch
- a compost heap
- a rock garden
- a pond
- a pile of rotted or rotting logs and branches.

You should also pay attention to the vertical aspects of your

Bluebells (Hyacinthoides non-scripta) *have been encouraged here to create a natural-looking carpet in a woodland garden. Native insects such as bumble-bees will be grateful for this nectar source early in the season.*

garden. If you plant a few trees and shrubs, these will offer hiding and nesting opportunities at a range of heights. When you dig a new flowerbed or a hole for a pond, heap the removed soil into a mound to create an additional landscape feature. This will automatically improve the wildlife diversity

11

because the slopes will have different microclimates that are attractive to different species. Woodlice, spiders, beetles and other invertebrates will quickly colonise the dark, damp sites, while the sunny slopes will attract basking butterflies and dragonflies.

The edges of planted borders should also be gently curving rather than ruler-straight. Not only will this look better, but the range of microhabitats will be increased, and hence also the diversity of wildlife.

Trees, shrubs and other plants

Trees are highly desirable – especially our own native species, which attract a host of useful and interesting animals. If possible, try to have a mixture of deciduous and evergreen trees, to ensure foliage throughout the year.

Holly is especially good – it provides permanent food and shelter for a range of species, including the pretty holly blue butterfly. If your holly tree is female, it will yield a crop of bright-red berries to provide food in the autumn and through the winter.

Rowan (Sorbus aucuparia) *is a native tree that is very easy to grow in the garden. It has attractive, feathery foliage, clusters of creamy-white flowers and (as here) produces copious quantities of red berries in the late summer and autumn, which will provide food for many birds.*

Birch and alder are also very good trees for wildlife as these will attract blue tits, goldfinches and redpolls, as well as being home to countless insects and spiders.

Exotic trees can also be beneficial, adding welcome structural variety and cover. But they are less likely to attract and support native wildlife. Certain exotic conifers with dense foliage, such as the notorious hybrid Leyland cypress (× *Cupressocyparis leylandii*), may have the advantage of rapid growth, providing privacy and also safe nesting sites, but otherwise do little to enhance the garden's biodiversity.

If space allows, it is good practice to plant a small grove of trees – for example, several birch trees in a group – thus mimicking a wood in miniature. Insects and birds in particular will respond well to this and make use of the interlocking foliage and cover.

If you are lucky enough to have established native trees such as oak or ash in your garden, these will act as a magnet for all types of wildlife; and it is also a good idea to plant some fruit-bearing trees such as rowan, cherry, apple or crabapple. Rowan is a particularly good choice (see picture below). Not only does it grow quickly and look good in any

An old stone wall can be a veritable treasure-trove of wildlife. The crumbling surfaces will be colonised by mosses, lichens and ferns, and the crevices will house invertebrates such as spiders, woodlice and beetles.

garden, it will also produce red berries in the autumn, which will be welcomed by birds.

Many garden birds use tall trees as song posts, and this is another good reason to include trees in your garden.

One of the finest wildlife gardens I know includes an old abandoned orchard that has been allowed to run wild. In amongst the gnarled trunks of the trees, lank grasses and wild flowers such as cow parsley, garlic mustard, clovers and vetches compete with patches of nettles and clumps of impenetrable bramble.

Each spring this magical grove hums to the sound of thousands of bees and other insects gathering nectar from the flowers, while blackbirds, blackcaps, wrens and robins feed and nest amongst the tangled growth. Then, in the autumn, the unharvested fruit drops to the ground or ripens on the trees – more food for the native wildlife. Foxes and muntjac occasionally scuttle through the undergrowth, finding welcome cover in this jungle.

Many of the old apple trees are clad in a thick growth of ivy, old man's beard or honeysuckle – food plants for adult and larval butterflies – while their stems offer niches for nesting birds.

Such areas are difficult of access but provide true havens for all kinds of wildlife, acting as reservoirs to enrich the adjacent more formal and open parts of the garden. What is more, this kind of wild garden is almost entirely maintenance-free.

If your garden is bounded by vertical walls, consider growing climbing plants up these, perhaps using a trellis as a support. Ivy will sometimes climb up walls and can also look attractive.

If you are planting a hedge along the edge of the garden, think about the composition of species. Ancient field boundary hedges were developed directly from the native trees and shrubs of old woodland, and therefore contain a range of native species such as blackthorn, hawthorn, bramble, rose, elder, guelder rose and honeysuckle. Ideally, this is the sort of hedge you should strive to encourage, as it will be much richer in wildlife than a hedge created from a single species. If you are planting with a single species, it may be worth using a shrub that produces a good crop of edible berries, such as firethorn. Remember that spiny hedge species will help to keep out undesirable visitors such as roe deer or muntjac.

Old, crumbly walls that have fallen into disrepair can be rich in small-scale wildlife. The stones may be encrusted with lichens and mosses, and ferns may grow in the cracks. The crevices will provide splendid retreats for spiders, woodlice and many other invertebrates, and possibly also for lizards,

The tall fronds of royal fern (Osmunda regalis) *provide dense cover for invertebrates and amphibians in a wet hollow or swamp garden. Here they make a splendid background for the showy flowers of ragged-robin* (Lychnis flos-cuculi).

paved, which is not recommended for a wildlife garden.

However, not all lawns are wildlife-friendly. At one extreme is the flat grass monoculture that is manicured and treated with regular doses of weedkiller to exclude all but grass so that it resembles some kind of green fabric, rather like the images on the packets of grass seed. Whilst this may be suitable for a bowling green, a cricket pitch or a tennis court, it is inappropriate for the wildlife garden.

At the other extreme might be a lush meadow of tall grass intermixed with meadow flowers, and rich in so-called 'weeds'. Many lawn 'weeds' such as clovers, dandelion and daisy have pretty flowers and establish themselves quickly from airborne seeds. Some gardeners are obsessed with excluding these and other species, and go to great lengths and expense to eradicate all but the lawn grass itself. Yet for the wildlife garden such species should be encouraged, in at least part of the lawn, as they attract insects.

Lawns are highly flexible and may be developed in various ways to create the maximum

voles and mice. So you should think twice before demolishing such ancient walls – it would take years to replace such an excellent wildlife habitat.

Cool, shady or north-facing areas could be candidates for a fernery. In some regions, notably in the north and west, ferns are a common feature of the woods and hedgerows, and may easily be encouraged to thrive in suitably damp spots in the garden. Always use native species such as hart's-tongue *(Phyllitis scolopendrium)*, male fern *(Dryopteris filix-*

mas), polypody *(Polypodium vulgare)*, or hard and soft shield ferns *(Polystichum aculeatum* and *P. setiferum)*. Ferneries not only look very good in the garden, they are home to many invertebrates as well as sheltering frogs, toads and newts.

Lawns

Most gardeners give at least part of their garden over to lawn, and indeed a garden is not easy to use unless it includes a reasonable stretch of grass – unless of course it is diversity. Part of the lawn, probably nearest the house, should be kept short and mown, partly as an amenity, but not least to provide a feeding site for blackbirds, thrushes and starlings that like to probe for worms.

Good advice is to allow one or more areas of lawn to turn into a meadow – a fascinating process to observe and one that will go a long way towards increasing the numbers of beneficial and attractive wildlife. Simply leave the grass uncut in certain areas until the

To encourage wildlife, at least part of the lawn should be left to grow into a meadow that will form a habitat for butterflies, grasshoppers and other small creatures.

grasses have reached their full height and maturity. Ryegrass *(Lolium perenne)* will reach about 90 cm (35 in), cock's foot *(Dactylis glomerata)* about 1 m (40 in), and these may be overtopped by taller grasses such as false oat-grass *(Arrhenatherum elatius)*. If you are lucky, you may find the beautiful nodding flowerheads of quaking grass *(Briza media)*, which grows to about 50 cm (20 in).

Such meadow areas should be mown on a regular cycle – once or more each season from midsummer onwards. Experiment with different cutting regimes and observe how this affects the species composition. If you have the space, mow different areas of

lawn at different times of the year. Varying the regime will create patches of different heights – visually attractive and offering a greater range of wildlife habitats. Eventually a range of flowers will establish themselves, including bird's foot trefoil, bladder campion, cowslip, self-heal, scabious, germander speedwell, knapweed, stitchwort, bedstraws, clovers and ragged robin. These in turn will attract still more insects such as butterflies and bees.

It is possible to introduce some flowers such as cowslips by planting so-called 'plugs' in amongst the grasses. If you are seeding a lawn afresh, then you could use a meadow mixture, which includes seeds

A green woodpecker (Picus viridis) *on a lawn. These fascinating birds have increased in recent years and find lawns to their liking. They spend a great deal of time there probing for ants, which they extract using their long tongues.*

of a range of suitable attractive meadow flowers with the grass seed. Meadows such as these will bring in many insects, including moths, beetles and grasshoppers as well as butterflies, and also provide cover for voles, field mice and frogs.

Water features

Arguably the single most successful way to increase the wildlife in your garden is to create a pond. Yet to design and construct the perfect wildlife pond is not easy.

The ideal pond combines areas of deeper open water with gently sloping, shallower reaches where fully aquatic plants can grade into swampy margins colonised by waterside species such as sedges, marsh marigold and yellow iris.

Unless you desire to keep fish in your pond – whether orna-

mental goldfish or koi carp, or less showy native species – it is best to leave native pondlife to arrive on its own. In this way you will end up with a rich aquatic fauna, including many important and fascinating invertebrates. The latter would

be eaten by fish save for a handful of pond snails.

Water beetles and water boatmen will fly into the pond on warm summer evenings and establish themselves quite naturally, and many other species will appear given time.

Introducing goldfish to a garden pond. This should be done gently, and only after the temperature of the water in the bag has been equilibrated to that of the pond. Bear in mind, however, that the fish will consume many of the native pond invertebrates, and may themselves fall prey to herons (see page 53).

Features of a wildlife pond

A shallow area provides a bathing spot for birds and an escape route for animals that fall in.

A bank with plenty of rocks and logs where frogs or newts can hide, while other creatures may bask on top.

A marginal zone planted with bog plants such as sedges, rushes, irises, marsh marigold and purple loosestrife – a haven for emerging dragonflies and damselflies.

Inside the deep-water zone, with floating-leaved plants such as frogbit above and a host of small creatures below such as a water boatman (top left), a dragonfly nymph (bottom left), a great diving beetle (centre) and several tadpoles.

A bog or swamp garden need not be devoid of colourful flowers. Here primulas intermingle with Mimulus *and* Iris *species.*

If your pond is large enough, dragonflies will breed, and their voracious larvae will lurk and grow amongst the aquatic plants.

A good plan is to include some rocks or stone slabs in or around the pond. Not only do these look good, they also give direct access to open water for birds and other animals for drinking or bathing.

The pond could be topped up using rainwater diverted from the downpipe of the house or shed, and in these times of water shortages this is a sensible option.

If your garden includes a poorly-draining area that seems always to be wet, then you could convert this into a bog or swamp garden by hollowing it out and planting, for example, sedges, rushes, marsh marigolds, yellow iris and purple loosestrife. Or you could install an artificial pond liner and fill it with damp soil before planting the swamp or bog species. Always bear in mind that some marsh plants such as great fen sedge (saw-sedge; *Cladium mariscus*) are very aggressive and can take over the entire area if you are not careful.

Most garden ponds attract frogs eventually, and if you are really lucky you may find that newts also take up residence – a sure sign of a healthy pond. But unless you have a pond that is close to open country, or the shelter of long grass or other vegetation, I would not recommend encouraging a breeding colony of frogs, fascinating though it is to watch the tadpoles develop into tiny froglets. A small pond can end up as a veritable tadpole soup, many of which die, and the frogs that survive need access to the safety of shelter as soon as they emerge from the water, with plenty of escape routes available.

Newts are far more suitable amphibians for most garden ponds, especially smaller ponds in modest gardens. Curiously, one cannot have both frogs and newts breeding. Newts are partial to frogspawn and soon displace the frogs. What is more, newts are more endangered than frogs and we can aid their conservation by allowing them to breed in our gardens.

Remember that newts spend quite a lot of time on land. In hot weather they may hole up in some damp crevice, and in the autumn they will seek out a sheltered spot to hibernate – under a log or stone, for example. So you should always place logs or rocks close to the newt pond in order to facilitate access both into and out of the water.

Habitats and micro-habitats for vertebrates and invertebrates

When creating a garden for wildlife, it is important to consider not just the overall shape and size of the garden and its major components, but to think also about the detailed aspects. The slightest altera-tions of angle or aspect, sun or shade, dampness or dryness, have a major influence on the wildlife. With a little thought you can create habitats within the garden to encourage particular animals. At the smaller end of the scale, such sites are often referred to as microhabitats.

The aim should be to offer as many different habitats as space will allow:

- trees and shrubs for birds
- dense patches of low-growing plants for small rodents, shrews and hedgehogs
- a pond for amphibians and other aquatic creatures
- open lawns for feeding birds, but also for hedgehogs and (with luck) badgers
- flowery borders as fuelling stations for bees and butterflies

… and so on. Try to make such varied habitats intergrade rather than ending abruptly with sharp borders between them. Not only does this look much better, it also encourages

A pile of rotting logs provides the ideal microhabitat for a host of small to medium-sized creatures.

19

the animals to move about more readily from one habitat to another.

While most of us desire a garden that looks reasonably tidy (without seeming fussily over-organised), the wild animal life – especially the invertebrates and smaller vertebrates – will benefit most if some areas of the garden can be left in a somewhat more natural state. In a wood, the accumulation of leaf litter, twigs and branches is part of the natural cycle and woodland creatures are adapted to thrive there. This means you should try to create similar conditions in some parts of the garden. Avoid the temptation to clear up leaf litter from under all the trees and shrubs, and make a pile of branches or logs in a quiet corner. This will rapidly be colonised by many invertebrates such as woodlice, spiders, centipedes and millipedes, nearly all of which will benefit the garden, and provide food for small mammals such as wood mice, voles and hedgehogs. Bumblebees seek out crevices and holes in which to nest, and wildlife gardens can play an important role in the conservation of this threatened group of insects.

Garden centres and specialist garden suppliers now offer a range of homes and shelters for garden insects and other invertebrates, as well as for hedgehogs and amphibians.

Thus you can buy ready-made hedgehog and frog shelters and a range of containers with tubular shelters for earwigs, bees and other insects. But you can easily make your own using logs, stones and small boxes.

An elaborate solution is to make a wildlife tower or hotel, using a stack of wooden pallets filled with a variety of sticks, stones, flower pots, bricks, hollow canes and the like. This can even be topped off with turf and planted with ivy and other species, and will offer a huge range of microhabitats, as well as being a conversation-piece! But a jumble of logs and brushwood will often do the job just as well.

This home-made wildlife apartment block provides a tremendous range of microhabitats within a relatively small area.

Alternatively, it could be incorporated within a wall or bank – less obtrusive yet just as effective.

The peacock is a common garden butterfly that often emerges early from hibernation. The adults feed from a wide range of flowers; the caterpillars favour nettles.

Garden butterflies

Gardens planned to be attractive to butterflies can play an important role in the conservation of these wonderful insects.

Many of our native butterflies have declined through loss of habitat in the wild (although the trend has been successfully reversed in the case of some species such as the Adonis blue). So we can all do our bit to protect and nourish those butterflies that visit gardens, mainly by growing plants that provide food for the caterpillars, as well as those with showy, nectar-rich flowers – refuelling stations for the adults.

Although they are delicate in build, butterflies can cover remarkable distances, and will often visit gardens even if these are some distance from their starting point. Indeed, several butterflies (and moths) are migrants that arrive here each summer from much further south, having flown distances comparable with some migrant birds. An example is the painted lady, which travels to Britain each year from North Africa and the Middle East.

In addition to the common whites (large, small and green-veined), the following species may reasonably be expected to turn up in gardens: small tortoiseshell, peacock, red admiral, comma, brimstone, orange tip, holly blue, painted lady, and also possibly speck-led wood and gatekeeper. If you have grassy areas, then you may also find meadow brown, common blue, small heath, and small and large skippers.

Attracting butterflies involves providing food plants for the adults, for the larvae (caterpillars) or for both.

Attracting adult butterflies
To attract adults it is best to plant a variety of nectar-rich species – preferably in a sunny spot – and to choose a range that will be flowering at different times of the year (see table below). Always plant tall species at the back of the bed, and lower-growing species

---

Nectar-rich flowers that attact butterflies

Spring-flowering	Summer-flowering	Autumn-flowering
Aubretia *(Aubrieta deltoides)*	Buddleia *(Buddleia davidii)*	Goldenrod *(Solidago virgaurea)*
Honesty *(Lunaria annua)*	Catmint *(Nepeta cataria)*	Helenium *(Helenium autumnale)*
Primrose *(Primula vulgaris)*	Globe-thistle *(Echinops sphaerocephalus)*	Hyssop *(Hyssopus officinalis)*
Sweet rocket *(Hesperis matronalis)*	Knapweed *(Centaurea nigra)*	Ice plant *(Sedum spectabile)*
Sweet violet *(Viola odorata)*	Lavender *(Lavandula spicata)*	Michaelmas daisy *(Aster novi-belgii)*
Wallflower *(Cheiranthus cheiri)*	Marjoram *(Origanum officinale)*	Sweet scabious *(Scabiosa atropurpurea)*
Yellow alyssum *(Alyssum saxatile)*	Mignonette *(Reseda odorata)*	Winter savory *(Satureia montana)*
	Red valerian *(Centranthus ruber)*	
	Thyme *(Thymus drucei)*	

towards the front – for example, buddleias at the back, with Michaelmas daisies, lavender, red valerian and knapweed in the centre, then the low-growing species such as catmint, thyme, primrose and aubretia at the front.

Encouraging butterflies to breed

This is more of a challenge in the garden, as it means providing a suitable habitat and the correct larval food plants. Female butterflies are very fussy about where they lay their eggs, and often spend a long time fluttering about seeking just the right chemical and visual clues before selecting a leaf or stem. It is also important to avoid using pesticides and other chemicals.

The food plants of some common garden butterflies are listed in the table on the right. Several species use nettles, so a nettle patch is a good idea. Butterflies often prefer to lay their eggs on young plants, so you should get into the habit of cutting down some of the nettles in mid-summer to encourage re-growth. A mixed meadow of various grasses is the best way to encourage the grass-breeding species.

Butterfly	Main larval food plants
Brimstone	alder buckthorn, buckthorn
Large white	brassicas, nasturtium, wild mignonette
Small white	brassicas, nasturtium, charlock, garlic mustard
Green-veined white	charlock, garlic mustard, hedge mustard, cuckooflower
Orange tip	cuckooflower, garlic mustard, honesty
Small tortoiseshell	nettle
Peacock	nettle
Red admiral	nettle
Painted lady	thistles, mallows, nettle
Comma	nettle, hop
Common blue	bird's-foot trefoil, black medick, restharrow, clovers
Holly blue	holly, ivy
Speckled wood	grasses: cock's-foot, false brome, Yorkshire fog
Gatekeeper	grasses: cock's-foot, couch, fescues, Timothy
Wall	grasses: cock's-foot, tor-grass, wavy hair-grass, Yorkshire fog
Meadow brown	grasses: fescues, bents, meadow-grasses, rye-grass
Small heath	grasses: fescues, bents, meadow-grasses
Small skipper	grasses: Yorkshire fog
Large skipper	grasses: cock's-foot, false brome, purple moor-grass

Ice plant (Sedum spectabile) is a firm favourite. The flowerheads consist of dense clusters of tiny nectar-rich flowers that are much appreciated by butterflies and other insects in the late summer and autumn.

Desirable and undesirable wildlife

A hedgehog house may attract one of these creatures to nest and hibernate in your garden. Place it in a quiet, sheltered position and put out plenty of nesting material nearby.

The general theme of this book is the creation of a garden that is pleasant and colourful while at the same time being attractive to wildlife. There are only a handful of plants that become troublesome 'weeds' – that is, 'plants in the wrong place' – and the same applies to animals, the majority of which are beneficial to the garden.

On the other hand, there are some animals that can be a real nuisance in the garden. Such problem species include deer, grey squirrel and a number of pest insects. The latter can often be controlled by encouraging their natural predators – thus aphids are eaten by ladybirds and lacewings – but for the mammals we may sometimes need to use more direct, 'unnatural' methods.

We shall first consider some of the useful wildlife, without which a garden would be a poorer place.

Hedgehogs are nocturnal hunters that emerge quietly at dusk to snuffle about for beetles, worms and other invertebrates. These much-loved animals can be encouraged by leaving piles of leaf litter and preparing suitable hiding places. They should not, however, be given bread and milk – it is not good for them.

Useful garden wildlife

This ladybird box can be hung from a tree. It will provide year-round protection for ladybirds, ensuring a thriving population to keep aphids at bay.

Which species can be regarded as positively useful in the garden? The short answer is that the majority of garden wildlife is 'useful' in the sense that the animals together create a balanced ecosystem. However, there are some species that stand out as especially beneficial. For more information on the individual species, please turn to the directory section of this book.

Birds

Many garden birds help to rid the garden of damaging insects and other invertebrates. Amongst the common garden birds that perform this valuable service are blue and great tits, robin, blackbird, song thrush, wren, blackcap and starling. Few birds cause actual damage in the wildlife garden.

Mammals

The most popular and useful garden mammal is undoubtedly the **hedgehog** (see previous page). Hedgehogs emerge at night and patrol the lawns, foraging amongst the shrubs and leaf litter as they hunt down beetles, slugs, worms, caterpillars and other larvae, many of which are harmful to garden plants.

Invertebrates

Ladybirds

Amongst the insects, ladybirds are definitely most welcome. Not only are they attractive, they also help by consuming large numbers of aphids. Both adult and larval ladybirds eat them, so they are much to be encouraged in any garden.

Britain has as many as 42 species belonging to the ladybird family, of which 24 are immediately recognisable as ladybirds (the others are

A lacewing (Chrysopa carnea) feeds on aphids. Both the adults and larvae of this common garden insect consume aphids and are therefore most welcome.

small and unspotted). One of the commonest garden ladybirds is the seven-spot (pictured on page 74).

Ground beetles
These fast-moving, agile hunters prey on other invertebrates, including slugs and snails. They are therefore mostly beneficial in the garden.

Devil's coach-horse
Another useful beetle, with a flexible body and powerful jaws for catching other invertebrates.

Lacewings
Delicate green insects with thin, veined wings, lacewings often come to lighted windows at night (see photo opposite). Both larvae and adults eat aphids, and they also feed on spider mites and whiteflies.

Hoverflies
These insects often visit garden flowers and help to pollinate them. The larvae of many species are important predators of aphids.

Bees and wasps
Bumblebees and honeybees (and also smaller solitary bees) help by pollinating flowers, while wasps (both social and solitary species) feed on a wide range of smaller insects.

Ichneumon wasps
Parasitic relatives of wasps. Some species help to control pest caterpillars (such as large and small white butterflies) by parasitising them, while others attack aphids.

Centipedes
Active carnivores with powerful jaws. Some species (notably *Lithobius forficatus* – see page 76) include slugs in their diet, thus helping to keep down numbers of these undesirable molluscs.

Spiders
Spiders employ a variety of strategies for catching their prey. The common garden spider catches flying insects in its web, while the zebra and wolf spiders jump on their prey on the ground; the crab spiders lie in wait and rely on their superb camouflage for surprising their quarry.

Woodlice
Small crustaceans with seven pairs of legs, woodlice generally live in damp places such as rotting wood or under stones, although the kind known as pill-bugs can stand drier conditions. While some woodlice graze on living plant tissues, their activities are mainly positive – they break down leaf litter to humus and thus enrich the soil.

Worms
Their burrowing is important in aerating the soil. They also enrich the soil by dragging down plant material to feed on it. In a compost heap, worms are one of the main agents recycling the plant remains and converting this to humus.

Worm composter
This device harnesses the efforts of earthworms to convert everyday kitchen waste into a liquid feed for your garden plants. The best worms for composting are *Eisenia foetida* (red worm) and *E. hortensis*. These are often found in old compost piles, but are different from the earthworms you would normally find in the ground. They reproduce quickly, thrive in confinement, and can eat more than their own weight in food every day! When you purchase red worms, one pound is all you need to get started.

Grey squirrel – friend or foe?

Many people have a great dislike for grey squirrels, often dismissing them as 'rats with bushy tails' or 'vermin'. There are many reasons for this, including the fact that they occasionally raid birds' nests and eat the eggs or nestlings – which made them unpopular with gamekeepers – and that they can damage young trees by eating the bark.

Much publicity has also been given to the fact that they have gradually ousted the native red squirrel, partly by competing for resources and partly by spreading a disease to which they, but not the reds, are immune. 'Alien invader kills off native Squirrel Nutkin' is an emotive headline indeed, but it is wiser to take a more balanced view.

Recent evidence shows that, although the grey has pushed the red out of much of mainland England, it has not so far penetrated most of Scotland, and where there are no greys, as on the Isle of Wight and Anglesey, reds are still fairly common, even in deciduous woods – and in a few areas the two seem

Grey squirrels are notoriously agile and persistent in their attempts to get at peanuts and other food provided for birds. Various truly squirrel-proof feeders are available, however.

to exist side by side. In some other mainland sites, such as parts of northern England, reds are mostly restricted to stands of conifers, on which greys are not so keen.

Most of Europe has only red squirrels, so we could regard ourselves as fortunate in having two squirrel species with contrasting lifestyles and habits. Perhaps if grey squirrels were native rather than introduced, most people would welcome them into their gardens.

It is certainly an impressive sight to see them clambering through the trees, leaping delicately from branch to branch on their aerial walkways, or running vertically straight up a tree trunk. They can leap about 1.5 m (4 ft) vertically and 4 m (10 ft) or more horizontally – impressive agility for a relatively small mammal. Their antics at the bird table can also be interesting and amusing, and one can even buy (or create) squirrel mazes with food as the prize – it is surprising how rapidly they can learn to solve these!

Many bird feeders are now squirrel-proof, and squirrels can also be kept away from the bird table by providing squirrel feeders as well.

If you live in an area which still has red squirrels, they too may be attracted to peanut feeders.

Dealing with problem wildlife

One way of enticing grey squirrels away from bird feeders is to provide a squirrel feeder too. Only a squirrel is capable of lifting the lid to get at the food.

A worry for the wildlife gardener is that some species may cause damage if encouraged into the garden. In fact there are surprisingly few problem plants and animals, and most of these are introduced species that have not evolved to co-exist with our own native flora and fauna.

So although most wildlife is beneficial, either directly by consuming pests or indirectly by helping to turn waste matter into fertile soil, there is a handful of species that sometimes cause problems, occasionally serious. The culprits are usually either invasive, introduced species or those that undergo a population explosion under certain conditions.

Methods of deterring unwanted wildlife include chemical, electronic and also physical barriers, including the careful planting of spiny hedges such as brambles and firethorn. Most problem species can be deterred using 'natural' methods of one sort or another, without resorting to poisons that can damage food-webs and reduce the numbers of useful species as well as the target pests.

Nuisance plants

In the plant kingdom certain exotic species stand out as candidates. Notable among these are:

- Japanese knotweed *(Fallopia japonica)*
- Himalayan balsam *(Impatiens glandulifera)*
- giant hogweed *(Heracleum mantegazzianum)*
- rhododendron *(Rhododendron ponticum)*.

But with the exception of Japanese knotweed (which can be a nuisance in the garden as it is very fast-growing and hard to control) these species mainly affect wild sites such as road-sides, river banks or woodland.

Animal pests

As for nuisance animals, popular opinion would put the following at top of their list of culprits: brown rat, grey squirrel, rabbit, magpie, carrion crow, jay, sparrowhawk and possibly heron. Yet in most gardens none of these poses a real problem, and with careful planning their effects can be reduced.

Birds

Whilst it is true that **magpies** (and jays) have increased in suburban gardens, it is unfair to blame them for the demise of songbirds. Two points in particular are relevant here:

1 Songbird populations remain healthy in most suburban areas – it is in the open, intensively farmed countryside where they have suffered the greatest decline.

2 Predation from magpies, crows and sparrow-hawks has little effect on suburban songbird numbers, the predators taking a surplus of young or unhealthy birds.

The real causes of the decline in certain species are the removal of hedgerows, the excessive use of agricultural chemicals, and a 'cleaner' weed-and grain-free countryside.

If you have visits from rabbits or deer, newly planted trees or shrubs can be protected by fitting a guard to prevent the bark being chewed.

Grey squirrels are active, acrobatic and omnivorous, plundering many types of bird feeder, and also taking eggs and young birds from their nests. They also sometimes chew the bark from young trees and shrubs. That said, many people enjoy watching their antics, and several modern bird feeders are squirrel-proof.

In the case of moles, we are only usually aware of their presence from the molehills they throw up from their networks of underground burrows. This is only really a problem in manicured, low-cut lawns, however.

It is probably best not to kill moles, as they do take pest larvae and also help aerate the soil – and you should certainly not use poisons. It is possible to protect sections of the garden from moles by creating a barrier of compacted soil in a trench – and electronic mole deterrent devices are available. However, unless you have a croquet lawn or bowling green in your garden, moles are best left to their own devices.

Deer

Roe deer *(Capreolus capreolus)* and muntjac *(Muntiacus reevesi)* can certainly damage garden plants by browsing on a surprising range of plants and by barking trees, but they can easily be excluded, at least in smaller gardens, by installing fencing or by planting spiny, impenetrable hedges such as bramble or firethorn.

Small mammals

There are two small mammals that can prove a nuisance in gardens: the grey squirrel *(Sciurus carolinensis)* and the mole *(Talpa europaea)*. Of these, the former is introduced and is common in most gardens except small urban plots, while the latter is native and much less frequent except in rural areas.

Domestic cats

Perhaps ironically, domestic cats are more of a threat to garden wildlife than any wild predators. Cats may be a big

Moles consume large numbers of earthworms but are seldom seen on the surface. Their normal method is to catch the worms as they appear in their underground burrows.

problem in some gardens, especially in terraces with narrow gardens, where the density of cats can be extremely high. They are not the natural enemies of our native birds, which are therefore rather vulnerable to them, and some cats certainly do take large numbers of garden birds, especially fledglings of species such as blackbirds.

Nevertheless, healthy populations of most songbirds seem to persist even in the face of predation by cats, though there is evidence to suggest that some species can be affected. The decline in common lizards may be partly due to cats.

A number of methods can be tried to discourage cats. Fitting a bell to the cat's collar may give birds enough warning when they stalk their prey, and electronic cat-scaring devices that emit high-pitched tones when a cat walks past can have

some effect. You can also buy repellents such as pepper powder, or pellets that produce a smell disliked by cats, but these are usually only a very temporary solution. Try to reduce the amount of bare soil or fine gravel in your garden, because cats will use such areas as a toilet, and once

they get into the habit it is difficult to persuade them to go elsewhere. Covering bare soil with cocoa shell mulch is also quite effective.

For the wildlife gardener, physical barriers are much to be preferred as opposed to chemical or more extreme solutions.

The scaredy cat plant, Plectranthus (Coleus) canina, produces an unpleasant odour rather like tom cat's urine, and this scares away cats. It is also said to be effective in deterring dogs and foxes too. With its blue flowers it could be a useful and attractive addition to the garden – especially if you have a problem with cats.

Greenfly can cause considerable damage to the buds of many garden plants, notably roses and honeysuckle. Their populations can increase very rapidly under favourable conditions.

Beetle pests

A recent insect invader is the **harlequin ladybird** *(Harmonia axyridis)*, which was introduced to North America and Europe to control aphids and is now becoming increasingly common in Britain. This aggressive species poses a threat to our native ladybird species, and may therefore reduce the number and diversity of our own aphid hunters.

Two other beetle species can be troublesome in the garden: the vine weevil and the scarlet lily beetle. The **vine weevil** *(Otiorhynchus sulcatus)* chews lumps out of leaves, attacking many species, including rhododendrons and *Euonymus*. The larvae are even worse, feeding on the roots and underground storage organs of many garden plants. In the wildlife garden they can be controlled by using the minute nematode worm *Heterorhabditis megidis*, which can be bought from several mail-order companies.

The **scarlet lily beetle** *(Lilioceris lilii)* attacks mainly lilies and fritillaries, causing serious defoliation. This affects the quality of the bulbs, and may prevent flowering the following year. This beetle is a serious pest in parts of southern England and parts of Wales,

Invertebrates

Amongst invertebrates, some species stand out as pests, notably aphids (when in dense colonies), slugs and snails, and the larvae of some **butterflies** – especially **large** and **small white** (*Pieris brassicae* and *P. rapae*).

Aphids

Unless you have a massive attack of aphids – on roses, for example – then sprays are not recommended. It is surely much better to encourage the aphids' natural predators to do the job of controlling their numbers.

north to Lancashire and Yorkshire. Any adults, eggs or larvae should be removed early in the season.

Slugs and snails

These molluscs can be a real pain. If you live in an area with calcareous soil, or if your garden is bordered by walls with lime-rich mortar, then snails can be a problem.

The use of poison such as slug pellets is to be discouraged as these can cause illness or even death in the slugs' natural enemies – notably hedgehogs.

One passive solution is to experiment with the plants you grow, encouraging those the snails dislike – in other words let the snails help you plan your garden and they will thus be gradually deprived of sustenance.

If ducks have access to your garden, from a large pond or stream, then snails will not be a problem. Ducks gobble them up, crushing the smaller snails in their bills and swallowing the larger ones whole.

My own garden suffers from snail attack, especially in wet weather. I find the best solution is to collect the snails regularly and relocate them to a site where they are not going to be a problem – in my case a wilder garden backing onto open fields. Of course this should only be done with the permission of the recipient, whose local song thrushes will also benefit!

Minor insect pests

Several garden insects cause minor damage to plants, but cannot normally be regarded as pests. These include froghoppers and leafhoppers, which are both types of true bug (Hemiptera).

Froghoppers feed mostly on native plants such as grasses and rarely cause much damage in the garden. These are the insects responsible for the

The scarlet lily beetle can be a serious pest of lilies and fritillaries, especially in southern Britain. Fortunately its bright colouring makes it easy to spot.

spittle-like froth (frogspit) on plant stems (for which reason they are sometimes called spittle-bugs). The young froghopper (nymph) creates the froth to protect itself.

Rather more troublesome are the **leafhoppers**. These resemble froghoppers but are smaller. Some of the 250 British species can cause unsightly pale blotches on leaves as they feed on the sap and destroy the green chlorophyll in the nearby sections of the leaf.

You can sometimes see rather precise semi-circular holes at the edges of leaves. This is the work of **leaf-cutter bees** (*Megachile* species). These are solitary bees (i.e. they don't form colonies) that nest on dead wood, and make their cells from neat slices cut out of the leaves of several plants, including unfortunately roses. But as they are few in number, the damage is seldom great and the bees more than make up for this through the pollination they carry out.

Leatherjackets are the larvae of certain species of cranefly (family Tipulidae). They take their name from the leathery texture of their skin. The adults are known as craneflies or 'daddy-long-legs', and we often see them over lawns or blundering into lighted windows. The adults are harmless, but the larvae of certain craneflies feed on the roots of crops and some garden plants, and sometimes damage lawn grasses in this way.

Directory of garden wildlife

This chapter provides a catalogue of species likely to be found in the garden, with brief notes on identification, habitat and food preferences (for more information about garden birds, refer to the companion volume in this series, *Gardens for Birds*).

Of course gardens vary enormously in shape, size, soil and location, and a garden adjacent to open country will attract a somewhat different set of wildlife from a tiny patch behind a city terrace. Yet all gardens contain at least some wildlife, and knowledge of the various groups will enhance our appreciation of our own green spaces.

A recent survey by the Royal Horticultural Society found that the nation's chart of the most favourite species or groups puts the hedgehog as the clear front-runner (see table on right).

**UK garden favourites
(in order of popularity)**

Hedgehog
Robin
Frog
Butterfly
Blackbird
Blue tit
Ladybird
Bee
Squirrel
Goldfinch
Fox
Bumblebee
Toad
Badger
Wren
Dragonfly
Long-tailed tit
Thrush
Newt
Great spotted woodpecker
Slow-worm
Green woodpecker
Bat
Pheasant
Song thrush
Nuthatch
Worm

*Recently voted third-favourite garden animal, the common frog (*Rana temporaria*) often appears as if by magic in a garden pond. Frogs need plenty of hiding places around the pond, and ideally access to grassy areas nearby.*

Mammals

Most of us are familiar with several mammal species in our gardens – notably squirrels, hedgehogs, mice and rats. Yet even the larger wild mammals are much harder to spot than birds. This is chiefly because many of them are nocturnal, so that their presence may go unnoticed.

Some mammals such as grey squirrels and deer are notori-

ous for the damage they sometimes do to trees and other
garden plants (see page 26).
Yet even these animals have
their own charm, and their bad
reputations are sometimes
greatly exaggerated.

Carnivores

Apart from the ubiquitous
domestic cat, which sometimes
lives in the wild, the carnivores
most often seen in gardens are
fox and badger.

Fox
Vulpes vulpes
This animal looks like a small
red-brown dog with black-
backed ears and a bushy,
white-tipped tail.

From being an animal of the
open fields, woods and countryside, foxes have increasingly
moved into suburbia in recent
decades, and are now frequent
visitors to gardens, especially
in the south and west. In many
cities, notably Bristol and
Brighton, they are often seen
trotting about the streets!

Foxes (like dogs) feed on a
huge range of food and often
raid dustbins for scraps. They
do little real damage in gardens
although they may burrow
under fences and sheds.

Badger
Meles meles
Badgers (pictured overleaf) are
low-slung and lumbering, with

*In recent years foxes have
become regular visitors to the
suburbs, turning up in gardens
and even, as here, resting in
garages and outhouses.*

grey fur and a striking black-
and-white face.

These animals are even more
nocturnal than foxes, and are
less often seen in gardens.
They are also much more
secretive and shy than foxes.
They do, however, enter
gardens where these adjoin
open country or woodland.

Although they will feed on a
wide range of food – from
fruits and berries to small
rodents – much of their diet is

33

in fact earthworms, and they therefore like to be close to grassland for feeding.

Badgers can cause problems in gardens by digging, but they are such magical animals that few begrudge them this.

Weasel and stoat

Mustela nivalis and *M. erminea*
The weasel and its larger relative the stoat are active carnivores that may be present in the garden, but are hardly ever spotted.

Badgers like to hunt for worms in gardens and they can be quite inquisitive, using their keen sense of smell to track down their food. Here a pair of badgers is inspecting a watering can.

They feed mainly on mice and voles, which they can hunt in their burrows. Thus they can be useful in the garden, as these small rodents can be a nuisance in sheds and store-houses by feeding on stored grain, birdfood and the like.

The male adult weasel is only about 25 cm (10 in) long, and the female just 18 cm (7 in), each with a tail of about 9 cm (3.5 in). Stoats are a little larger than weasels, the male being 30 cm (12 in) and female 25cm (10 in) long, with a tail of about 12 cm (4.5 in). Another difference is that stoats have a black tip to the tail and (in northern or high-altitude regions) turn white or partly white in winter.

Stoats eat small rodents but also kill rabbits and chickens, so they can be a potential threat if you keep poultry.

Deer

Only two species of deer are regularly seen in and around gardens – the native roe deer and the introduced muntjac.

Roe deer

Capreolus capreolus
Roe deer are native to the British Isles. Although mostly found in woodlands, these deer are seen occasionally in urban areas, but they are nocturnal and very shy by nature, so are only likely to enter larger gardens and parkland areas.

If your garden adjoins woodland or open country, you may spot a roe deer, especially around dawn or dusk. Deer browse on garden plants and can be a nuisance, but they are usually seen only rarely in gardens.

Muntjac
Muntiacus reevesi

These deer originated in Asia, but since their escape from Whipsnade Zoo and Woburn Park, they have spread widely in central and southern England. Feeding on grass, tree bark and a wide range of plants, they can cause considerable damage to gardens and are particularly fond of roses!

Muntjacs have reddish-brown coats with a short tail with a white underside, which can be seen when the deer runs away. The male has short spiky antlers.

Rabbits and hares

Rabbit
Oryctolagus cuniculus

In large gardens, rabbits can play a useful part in a balanced ecosystem, cropping large areas of grass and fertilising it with their droppings.

However, in smaller gardens they are often considered pests on account of the large amount of damage they can do in a relatively short space of time! They feed mostly on grass, but occasionally eat tree bark too, and can therefore cause considerable damage to garden plants.

Renowned for their rapid breeding, rabbits produce up to five litters a year, nesting in underground burrows. They can be most effectively excluded by fencing (see page 28).

Hare
Lepus europaeus

Hares are larger than rabbits, sporting distinctive long, black-tipped ears and longer legs. They are essentially animals of the open fields, having eyes on the sides of their heads to give them all-round vision. They are rarely seen in gardens, and only then if there are fields nearby.

Hares have an exclusively vegetarian diet, eating mainly grasses.

The charming wood mouse, sometimes called the long-tailed field mouse, is a lively rodent and is often found in gardens. Although wood mice sometimes feed on stored seeds and grain, they usually do little damage, feeding on a wide range of wild fruits, seeds and invertebrates.

Red squirrel
Sciurus vulgaris
The smaller red squirrel (pictured on page 26) has tufted ears and red-brown fur. It feeds mostly on pine kernels, seeds, nuts and other vegetable matter. It is now extinct in much of the British Isles, though still widespread in Europe, appearing regularly in parks and gardens. Apart from a few isolated populations such as on the Isle of Wight and Anglesey, the red squirrel is now only found commonly in Scotland and adjoining parts of England, often in areas of coniferous forest.

Brown rat
Rattus norvegicus
Brown rats are sometimes found in gardens, especially in rural areas where there is stored grain or other food, or close to ponds and streams. They swim well and in many places have displaced water voles from streams and rivers. They can cause damage by gnawing and burrowing; this, together with their habit of raiding stores, has made them unpopular, but they do little damage to plants and flowers.

Rodents
Rodents specialise in gnawing their food, and have sharp, chisel-teeth. They range in size from agile squirrels to the tiny harvest mouse.

Grey squirrel
Sciurus carolinensis
The grey squirrel (see page 26) was introduced to Britain from North America in the late 19th century, since when it has largely displaced the native red squirrel. Grey squirrels feed on a wide range of vegetable matter together with insects and small animals. They are particularly prominent in sub-urban areas and feed regularly at bird feeders. Although often amusing in their antics, grey squirrels do considerable damage through tree barking, and they also take eggs and nestlings from birds' nests.

House mouse
Mus domesticus

Despite their name, house mice are often found in gardens, especially in sheds and outhouses. They are generally greyer than the wood mouse, and are nearly always associated with human activity. They can become a nuisance as they attack stored edible material of all kinds and leave droppings.

Wood mouse (Long-tailed field mouse)
Apodemus sylvaticus

Much livelier than the house mouse, and larger and paler, with a longer tail, wood mice also jump and climb well, and sometimes use old birds' nests as storage sites for berries. Wood mice are welcome garden guests. They do not usually damage stored grain, and they will sometimes come to low-level feeding tables.

Harvest mouse
Micromys minutus

This tiniest of our mice is a true charmer! It is only about 6 cm (2.5 in) long with a 2-cm (1-in) prehensile tail, which it uses to help cling to grass stems and thin twigs.

The favoured habitat is rough hedges and reedbeds. In

The harvest mouse is now something of a rarity, but if your garden is close to rough pasture, or especially reedbeds, you may be lucky enough to host this delightful small rodent.

earlier times they were often found in wheat crops – hence the common name – but modern harvesting methods and 'cleaner' crops have diminished populations in these traditional sites. Harvest mice build spherical nests attached to the stems of stout grass, wheat or reed.

Bank vole
Clethrionomys glareolus

Often the first (or only) sign that bank voles are in the garden is a network of tunnels near or at the surface through the grass and vegetation. They are very secretive and hard to spot. Bank voles are very welcome in gardens, where they feed on seeds, berries, nuts and also invertebrates. Their natural habitats are woods and hedgerows.

Field vole (Short-tailed vole)
Microtus agrestis

Mainly an animal of open fields, meadows and pasture,

A common dormouse feeds on hawthorn. Its alternative name of hazel dormouse indicates its close association with hazel, the nuts of which are a favourite food, though it is also partial to many fruits. Like most small mammals, hazel dormice are nocturnal and very hard to spot.

vegetable matter, particularly hazelnuts.

Hazel dormice are relatively slow-moving, but are agile climbers. They are nocturnal and hibernate among tree roots or in burrows. In gardens they can be encouraged to nest in artificial boxes.

Edible dormouse
Glis glis
Rather like miniature grey squirrels, these creatures sport a well-furred grey tail and large, dark eyes.

Their name refers to the Roman fashion for eating them as a delicacy. Introduced into England from continental Europe in 1902 (they escaped from a collection at Tring in Hertfordshire), edible dormice are still mainly confined to the

the field vole is greyer than the bank vole. It can occur in gardens, especially where these adjoin open country and have areas of long grass.

Water vole
Arvicola terrestris
Much larger than our other voles, and the size of a small rat, water voles (in Britain at least) are only found near clear rivers, streams and sometimes in large ponds. Their numbers have crashed since the spread of introduced mink, which are very partial to water voles.

Now that otters are spreading again and replacing mink, there are signs of a revival in water vole populations. If you have a large pond or stream in your garden, you may be lucky enough to attract these charming animals.

Hazel dormouse (Common dormouse)
Muscardinus avellanarius
One of the prettiest rodents, these dormice are dark orange with large eyes and a furry tail. Found mostly in rural places, they feed on insects and

Britain's favourite garden animal, the hedgehog, may be encouraged by supplementary feeding, or by leaving bowls of drinking water in hot weather. Although hedgehogs will eat slugs, their main diet consists of beetles and caterpillars. Do not give them bread and milk as it disagrees with them, but tinned dog or cat food is suitable.

Chilterns within about 25 miles of Tring, but are slowly spreading and now number about 10,000.

Edible dormice feed on a range of nuts, berries, insects, grubs and plant matter.

Insect eaters

Shrews, hedgehog and mole belong to a group known as insectivores because they feed mainly on invertebrates such as worms and insects.

Common shrew
Sorex araneus
Feeding on insects, earthworms and other invertebrates, as it name suggests this is the most commonly encountered

shrew. Light brown above and grey underneath, these shrews have velvety fur.

Artificial nesting can be encouraged in gardens, and shrews help by killing a range of pest invertebrates. They are hunted by birds of prey such as barn owls, and also killed by cats, which usually find them unpalatable.

Pygmy shrew
Sorex minutus
These shrews are similar to common shrews in appearance, but are distinguishable by their proportionately longer tails and slightly darker coats. They share the same diet as common shrews, and their

presence in gardens can similarly be encouraged. They breed underground, inside hollow logs or in grass-lined nest boxes, and have up to four litters a year.

Water shrew
Neomys fodiens
These fascinating shrews are found mostly near ponds and streams, feeding on small fish and other small animals.

When they dive, water shrews appear silvery in colour on account of the air trapped in their black fur. They rarely stay submerged for long, but emerge into riverbank tunnels, where water is squeezed from their fur.

Some species of bat such as the common pipistrelle may be encouraged to roost in a bat box. The best place for a bat box is high on a tree trunk, though the wall of a house may also be suitable.

Water shrews can be found some distance from streams, and they can be encouraged by leaving planks, logs or sheets of corrugated iron near a garden pond.

Hedgehog
Erinaceus europaeus

Our only spiny mammal is covered with as many as 7,000 sharp modified hairs. Voted our favourite garden animal, the hedgehog is unmistakable (pictured on previous page).

Hedgehogs eat slugs, snails, caterpillars and beetles, and do not harm plants – for these reasons they are universally approved of by gardeners. They are active at night and can travel 2–3 km (1.5–2 mi) in search of food.

In the late autumn they will be searching for somewhere to hibernate, so make sure you have plenty of shelter, such as log piles or undisturbed leaf litter. Remember to check bonfire stacks before lighting them, and transfer any hedgehogs you find to a safe site such as a hedgehog box.

Mole
Talpa europaea

Rarely seen above ground (except when dead), moles are easily distinguishable by their velvety black fur, pointed pink snouts and large front paws (see picture on page 29).

Keen diggers, moles are often considered pests by gardeners on account of their tendency to create molehills of dug soil. They feed on earthworms and insect grubs, and their tunnelling often helps to maintain drainage and fertility in soil. Their young are born in underground nests, blind and naked.

Bats

Of the 17 species of native bat, about five may be spotted in or around gardens. All of them feed on insects caught on the wing, and they do much to reduce the numbers of irritating flies, including midges and mosquitoes, although they also take large numbers of moths. In the winter they hibernate, in holes in trees, roof spaces or sometimes in bat boxes.

The presence of bats is usually a sign of a healthy environment, as they are very sensitive to chemicals and disturbance, and are encouraged by a wildlife-friendly garden.

Bats are the major predators of night-flying insects – one bat can catch more than 100 insects in just one hour's hunting. This can benefit the garden, as many of the insects consumed by the bats produce larvae that can damage flowers and vegetables.

Common pipistrelle
Pipistrellus pipistrellus

The smallest of all European bats, measuring 32–51 mm (12.5–20 in), and the commonest in Britain, pipistrelles are difficult to spot because they hide in small crevices in roofs. They prefer clean, dust-free environments, so are commonly found in the gardens of new houses, where they will sometimes use bat boxes if these are provided. Pipistrelles feed exclusively on flying insects, so if you stop using pesticides, this will encourage them.

Brown long-eared bat
Plecotus auritus
As their name suggests, these bats are distinguishable by their large ears, which they curl up when at rest. They are found fairly often in gardens and may roost in houses, where they may be seen hanging free or against a wall near the roof. They feed on insects and spiders, which they catch in flight. Relatively slow flyers, they can occasionally be seen hovering and picking insects off trees.

Noctule
Nyctalus noctula
These large bats have declined in many areas due to the felling of the hollow trees in which they like to roost. They have large ears, albeit not as large as those of the long-eared bats, and dark-orange fur.

Although mostly found in woodland areas, noctules will also roost in houses; they have been found in hollow concrete street lights and under bridges. Hunting in the early dawn and at dusk, noctules prey on moths, cockchafers and other larger flying insects.

Daubenton's bat
Myotis daubentonii
These medium-sized bats inhabit predominantly flat countryside and woodland areas, usually near water, and are even occasionally caught accidentally by anglers. Summer roosts have been found in attics, walls and under bridges, though rarely in bat boxes.

Daubenton's bats are dark grey or light brown in colour, but there have also been recorded cases of albinism. Their speedy wing-beat enables them to hunt low above water surfaces, feeding as they fly.

Natterer's bat
Myotis nattereri
These medium-sized bats can be found in both rural and urban areas. They roost in small groups, occasionally with Daubenton's bats, but hibernate later than the latter, from October to April.

Natterer's bats have relatively large ears, visible snouts and a pale belly. They feed by picking small insects and flies off leaves and other surfaces.

The noctule is one of our largest bats. It can sometimes be spotted hunting for moths and other insects over gardens, especially where there are large trees present.

41

Birds

We include here just a selection of the birds most likely to be seen in your garden. Birds such as the blackbird, wren, chaffinch or woodpigeon are unlikely to be absent from any garden. For more detailed information about garden birds, consult the companion title, *Gardens for Birds*.

Birds are unpredictable, and many unusual species may appear in the garden from time to time. The hints offered elsewhere in this and the companion book will help you to increase the number and variety of birds coming into your garden, whatever type of garden you have.

Species such as the lovely spotted flycatcher have virtually vanished both from our gardens and from the wider countryside, while others, including green woodpecker and blackcap, have now become commoner. Even the sly and stately grey heron can often be spotted gliding and spiralling down to a garden pond, especially in the early hours, and particularly if the pond is stocked with juicy fish!

Newcomers are not always welcomed though, and this is probably true of magpies, which have invaded suburban gardens in recent years. But all these add to the variety of our garden birds, and each species is interesting in its own way.

Birds benefit from a well-planted and varied garden with a good mix of trees, shrubs and herbs. It is important to provide safe cover for nesting, and plenty of species that produce edible berries or seeds. The range of feeders, tables and other equipment for

Robins are ever-present in all but the smallest gardens. In autumn they start to sing their rather mournful territorial songs. Their harmless appearance belies their nature – in fact they can be very aggressive, and fight hard when seeing off rivals.

garden birds is now extensive, as is the variety of food available through garden centres and specialist suppliers.

Remember that nearly all gardens, whether they be large or tiny, can be made more attractive to wild birds, and that this will help to make the garden a more fascinating and welcoming environment, as well as helping to conserve the birds themselves. Moreover, a healthy bird population will also help to reduce harmful insects and other pests in the garden, thus reducing the need to rely on chemical weedkillers or pesticides.

Although pressures on garden birds seem high – from domestic cats and magpies, for example – in fact gardens are highly productive, supporting large numbers of birds despite the activities of these predators, and they usually offer relatively safe nesting sites.

Predatory species such as squirrels, crows, magpies and sparrowhawks include young birds in their diets, and attacks on garden birds can be distressing. However, there is actually little evidence that they reduce urban and suburban populations of songbirds. The birds just seem to produce more offspring and make up

the losses. The presence of sparrowhawks, for example, is evidence for the existence of a healthy food chain, from garden invertebrates, through songbirds, to the hawks themselves. The latter are small in number in the garden ecosystem, although they may occasionally make dramatic appearances.

Woodpigeon
Columba palumbus
Our largest pigeon is very bulky, with a white patch on the neck and obvious white wing patches in flight. The call is a very pleasant long cooing,

with many syllables, ending abruptly.

This very common bird is found increasingly in gardens, where it can sometimes be a nuisance, feeding on vegetable crops. Woodpigeons look somewhat ungainly as they waddle about the lawn, searching for scraps or seeds dropped from feeders.

Feral pigeon
Columba livia
The common small 'pigeon' found in most cities and towns has descended from the wild rock dove. It comes in a wide range of colours and patterns,

A blackbird feeds on crabapples. A garden well stocked with berry-bearing trees and shrubs will attract wild birds, especially in the autumn and winter when wild food sources are diminishing.

43

although most retain the white rump of the ancestral form. It is found in city streets, parks and gardens, but also in the open countryside and on sea-cliffs, where it sometimes interbreeds with pure wild rock doves. It eats seeds and scraps of all sorts.

Collared Dove
Streptopelia decaocto

This small dove has pale grey-beige plumage, an incomplete black, white-edged collar and a white tip on the tail that is most noticeable in flight. The song is a cooing of three sylla-bles, accented on the second, which can sound cuckoo-like if half-heard or incomplete.

First recorded in Britain in the early 1950s, the collared dove is now one of our com-monest garden birds. It thrives best near human habitations, and is often seen in gardens, where it regularly visits bird tables to feed on seeds.

Tawny owl
Strix aluco

Our commonest owl can often be detected from its calls – a familiar drawn-out, tremulous hoot and a sharp 'kee-wick'. The brown, dappled plumage, combined with its strictly nocturnal habits, makes it very

hard to spot. Thus tawny owls are more often heard than seen, especially in late autumn when they are establishing their territories.

Tawny owls are found in wooded gardens and parks, and will sometimes make use of large nest boxes. They feed on small mammals, but may also take roosting birds and even earthworms from lawns.

Green woodpecker
Picus viridis

This chunky, rather wild-eyed woodland bird (see opposite) is increasingly seen in gardens in the neighbourhood of trees or heathy areas, especially if there are large lawns. The

bright-green plumage with a yellow rump (obvious in flight) makes a splendid sight. The flight is bounding and some-what heavy. The loud laughing 'yaffle' call carries a long way.

Green woodpeckers like nothing better than grubbing for ants – and lawns, especially on light, sandy soils are ideal for this purpose. These birds need old trees for nesting (by excavating a hole), combined with open ground for feeding.

Great spotted woodpecker
Dendrocopos major

Our commonest woodpecker is thrush-sized, with black-and-white plumage and red under the base of the tail. The large

A couple of tawny owl chicks stare out from their nest in a hollow tree. This woodland species has adapted well to garden life, but needs old trees in which to roost and breed.

Although normally seen hunting for ants on the garden lawn, green woodpeckers sometimes feed on windfall apples, as do many other garden animals.

hite patches on the back are istinctive and the flight is ndulating. This is the wood- ecker responsible for loud rumming on a hollow tree in ıe breeding season.

A bird of woodland, copses nd parkland, this woodpecker increasingly seen in gardens, here it sometimes visits eding stations. It feeds on ısects, especially those in ood or bark, supplemented nainly in winter) by fat and ther food from bird tables.

wift
Ipus apus

his fast-flying bird has black- h-brown plumage, a pale hin, long, sickle-shaped wings nd a shallowly forked tail. wifts spend most of their life n the wing, often for weeks at stretch outside the breeding eason. Screaming parties of everal birds display in the ımmer, sometimes circling to great height in the evenings. Swifts usually arrive in early lay and start to leave in mid- ugust. They nest mostly nder the eaves of houses, hurch towers and the like special swift nest boxes are lso available). Though not rictly speaking garden birds, wifts are a common sight over ardens, where they catch ısects on the wing.

Swallow
Hirundo rustica

Slim and elegant, with a long tail and fine streamers, swal- lows are metallic blue above with a red-brown chin and forehead. Young birds have shorter tails.

Swallows arrive in April, and nest mainly in farm buildings, stables, sheds or under bridges. The nest is an open cup made of grasses and mud.

Swallows often feed at low levels, hunting insects in smooth, flowing flight. They sometimes fly low over water, dipping their beaks to sip from the surface of a pond. They tend to hunt above meadows, pastures and areas of water, but are often seen around gardens, especially if there are outbuildings providing access for nesting.

House martin
Delichon urbica

This bird is smaller and more compact than a swallow, with metallic blue-black plumage above, pure white below and an obvious white rump. The tail is much less deeply forked. The flight is different too, being more fluttery, interspersed with glides. House martins usually hunt for insects at higher levels than swallows.

House martins arrive around mid to late April. They usually nest on buildings, including under the eaves of houses, in small or large colonies. The nest is a sealed dome of mud with an entrance hole at the side. They may sometimes be attracted into using a special nest box.

Pied wagtail
Motacilla alba
Our most familiar wagtail has black-and-white plumage and a long black tail with white outer tail feathers; the legs are also long and black. The flight call is a rather coarse double note: 'chiss-ick'.

Pied wagtails are common birds, and are found in most habitats except woodland. In gardens they may often be seen feeding on lawns, sometimes flying up to chase flying ants or other insects.

Wren
Troglodytes troglodytes
The tiny, rotund wren is one of our smallest birds. The short tail is often held cocked upright, and the flight is direct, with rapid wingbeats. The song is a rich warble, with many trills – surprisingly loud for such a small bird. The alarm call is a robin-like 'teck-teck', sometimes slurred.

Wrens construct domed nests, usually well hidden – often in ivy or among the root of a tree – though they sometimes nest in the corner of a little-used shed. They can be rather secretive and are usual spotted as they flit at low level from bush to bush.

Despite being one of our commonest birds, wrens suffe badly in really hard winters, and may huddle together for warmth on cold nights (over 60 have been found together in a single nest box). They are found in most habitats, from dense woodland to heaths, parks and gardens. They main ly eat small insects, spiders an other invertebrates.

Dunnock
Prunella modularis
The dunnock is also known as hedge sparrow, but it is not a true sparrow. In shape it rathe resembles a robin, with its thin bill. The head and breast are a slaty grey, the plumage otherwise brown and streaked.

Though common and widespread in gardens, dunnocks are easily overlooked. They ar birds of woodland and parks,

The wren is found in most habitats, including gardens. For its size it has one of the loudest and most penetrating of songs, and the strident trilling of a wren in full song is usually the first sig of its presence.

A robin in winter – a Christmas card cliché, but welcome all the same in any garden!

and tend to lurk in the foliage, making forays to feed in the open. Their diet includes mainly insects and seeds. They usually feed on the ground, often picking up fallen scraps from below a bird table.

Dunnocks have a complex and fascinating sex life, some males mating with more than one female, some females with more than one male.

Robin
Erithacus rubecula

Probably our best-known garden bird, the robin adorns many a Christmas card and catalogue. Both sexes have the distinctive orange-red breast, and their feisty behaviour makes them easy to spot. The song, delivered in autumn as well as spring, is a somewhat melancholy, descending series of rippling notes.

Robins prefer mature deciduous woodland, but are also found in hedgerows, parks and gardens. They eat mainly seeds and insects, but sometimes fruit, especially in winter. In the garden they may become quite tame, sometimes following the gardener and picking insects from freshly dug soil.

Song thrush
Turdus philomelos

This small thrush has brown upperparts and is pale cream and white below, speckled with clear dark spots. One of our loudest and finest songsters, its repertoire is essentially made up of short, fluted phrases, each repeated two or more times, and usually delivered from a high perch. The alarm call is a sharp 'tick-tick-tick'.

Although widespread, the song thrush has declined steadily in recent years, possibly because of pesticides and also habitat loss. It lives in woodland, parkland, meadows and heathland as well as gardens, and its food ranges from invertebrates (notably worms) to berries and fruits. It is well known for its ability to extract the flesh from snails after bashing them against a stone 'anvil' to break the shell. A collection of broken snail shells around a hard object is a sure sign that song thrushes are around.

Redwing
Turdus iliacus

Redwings are slightly smaller and darker than song thrushes, with a white stripe over the eye and a streaked rather than a spotted breast. The name comes from the bright red-brown flanks and inner under-wing. They have a very distinctive flight call – a high-pitched 'tsweep' – and flocks can be heard calling as they arrive in the autumn, often at night.

The redwing is a regular winter visitor from Scandinavia, but breeds occasionally in northern Scotland. A bird of open country, ploughed fields, pasture and playing fields, it also likes hedgerows, especially where there are berries, and in cold weather it will often come into gardens to feed on berry-bearing trees or shrubs such as holly or apples.

Mistle thrush
Turdus viscivorus
The mistle thrush is the largest of the European thrushes. Greyer than song thrush, it also has longer wings and tail, and larger spots on the breast. The white outer tail feathers are obvious in the heavy, undulating flight. The flight call is a buzzing 'tzrrr', and the song a wild, melancholy fluting, similar to that of the blackbird. Mistle thrushes start singing early in the season, often in February, and even during inclement weather, nearly always from a prominent position high in a tree.

Like the song thrush, the mistle thrush has suffered a steady decline in recent years. It lives in woodland, wooded pasture, parkland and large gardens, and feeds mainly on invertebrates, but will also take berries and other fruits.

Blackbird
Turdus merula
One of our commonest and most prominent garden birds, and instantly recognisable, the adult male being jet black with a yellow bill, the female brown, and young birds a rather russet brown. Some individuals show white flecks.

The blackbird's song is one of our finest – very clear, loud, and tuneful. The alarm call is a metallic 'tsink-tsink' or a chatter. The blackbird is found in woodland, hedgerows, parkland and gardens. It eats mainly insects and worms, but also seeds, fruits and scraps.

Blackcap
Sylvia atricapilla
The blackcap is a common warbler, easily identified by the black (male) or chestnut-brown (female) cap. The underside is pale and the back grey-brown. The song is a musical warbled phrase, the last section of which rises distinctly in pitch.

Blackbirds spend much time and energy in the breeding season laboriously collecting worms, caterpillars and other grubs to feed their growing broods.

Blackcaps live in open woodland, parks and gardens, and have grown steadily in numbers over recent decades. They increasingly overwinter in Britain, especially in mild winters. In spring and summer they eat mainly invertebrates, but are partial to berries and fruit in autumn and winter.

Chiffchaff
Phylloscopus collybita

One of our smallest warblers, with dull olive-brown plumage, a pale underside and dark legs and feet, the chiffchaff can usually be identified from its highly distinctive song – a monotonous, irregular repetition of two notes: 'chiff-chaff-chiff-chiff-chaff…'.

Widespread in areas with trees and woodland, chiffchaffs are mainly summer visitors, but some will overwinter, especially in the south. They mainly eat insects and spiders from high in the trees, but occasionally eat fruits in autumn and winter.

Willow warbler
Phylloscopus trochilus

This small warbler has greenish-yellow plumage, and is so similar to the chiffchaff that the two species are hard to distinguish unless they are heard singing. The song, however, could not be more different from the chiffchaff's: a descending series of clear notes, rising towards the end.

Though widespread, the willow warbler has declined in numbers since the late 1980s. Its habitat ranges from woodland, parks and gardens to fen willow and alder scrub, and heathy birch woodland. It feeds on insects and spiders,

Blackberries and rose hips should be left to ripen on the shrubs, where they will both brighten the garden and provide food for small mammals, squirrels and many birds.

which are usually taken high in the trees, though sometimes from the air.

Goldcrest
Regulus regulus

Our smallest bird (with the rarer firecrest) is dumpy, tiny and very pretty with olive-green plumage. The male has a bright-yellow crown, edged orange-red; the female's crown is light yellow. Goldcrests are fairly approachable, but often hard to see as they typically flit about in the branches of a conifer. The song is a high-pitched, rather tinkling phrase.

Goldcrests are widespread in parks and gardens where conifers are present. They build a delicate nest woven into the tip of a branch, using moss, fine wool and spiders' webs. They feed on tiny insects and spiders, which they usually pick from the foliage.

Spotted flycatcher
Muscicapa striata
Slim and lively, but with rather drab brown-grey plumage and a pale, streaked breast, the spotted flycatcher was once a common sight in parks, gardens and open woodland. One of our most delightful garden birds, its feeding behaviour is really fascinating to observe. It sits still on a prominent perch and makes repeated swooping flights to catch insects in the air. In cool weather it will also pick insects from foliage.

This bird has sadly suffered a serious steady decline since the 1970s. The reasons for this are unclear, but are perhaps related to changes in agriculture and the loss of large trees, combined with unfavourable conditions in wintering areas in southern and western Africa.

Long-tailed tit
Aegithalos caudatus
This bird is very small, but has a long, narrow tail that makes up more than half its total length, giving it a lollipop-like appearance, especially in flight. It is mainly black and white above, and pale white and pink beneath.

The long-tailed tit often travels about in family groups, and in flocks in winter, sometimes mixing with other tits. Birds usually keep up constant high-pitched contact calls when moving about. Communal

It is a good idea to hang food, such as this nut-enriched fat cake, from the branch of a tree or shrub, where birds like this blue tit can feed in relative safety.

roosts are common, especially in cold weather.

This tit is common in parks, gardens and woodland with rich undergrowth. It feeds on small insects and spiders, and creates a beautifully crafted oval nest incorporating feathers, lichens and spiders' webs.

Blue tit
Parus caeruleus
As one of our commonest and prettiest garden birds, the blue tit hardly needs describing. It is small, with blue-and-yellow plumage, and quite bold and aggressive at bird tables and feeding stations; it is often the first bird species to arrive at a new feeder.

Even birds such as the great tit that eat mainly insects will welcome the occasional peck at fruit like these ripe crabapples.

The blue tit likes woodland, especially where oak is present, but is also very common in parks and gardens, where it frequently uses nest boxes. While its natural diet is made up of insects and spiders, it is also very keen on peanuts, fat-balls, seed and other scraps.

Great tit
Parus major

The largest of our tits, the great tit is also one of our commonest birds. It has a black-and-white head, green back, yellow underparts and a black stripe down the centre of its belly – broad in the male and narrow in the female. The song is varied – often a simple repeated 'tea-cher, tea-cher ...' - starting very early in the year. Great tits often use nest boxes, and regularly visit bird tables and peanut feeders. Apart from insects (especially caterpillars) and spiders, they take a wide range of offered food such as peanuts, fat and seeds.

Nuthatch
Sitta europaea

This rather odd-looking bird is dumpy and woodpecker-like, with a short tail and a powerful chisel-shaped bill. It is blue-grey above, and creamy yellow or rusty beneath.

Nuthatches are very agile and can climb up, across or even down tree branches and trunks with ease. Their loud, liquid calls are distinctive – 'tvit-vit-vit-vit'. They nest in natural tree holes or old woodpecker holes, reducing the entrance size to exclude larger birds by daubing the edges with mud until the required diameter is achieved.

Though widespread and increasing in numbers, nuthatches are not so common in less-wooded areas. They are particularly fond of old trees, especially oak. They mainly eat insects, but also take nuts and seeds from feeders and tables, especially in cold weather.

Jay
Garrulus glandarius

This colourful member of the crow family is rather large and somewhat plump. In flight it is conspicuous, with its black tail, white rump and white and blue wing patches. The rest of the body is a cinnamon or pinkish colour. Jays make a

51

The ring-necked (rose-ringed) parakeet (Psittacula krameri) *is native to Asia, but has become established close to a number of cities, notably in some south London suburbs, where colonies breed in hollow trees. You may be lucky and see this exotic bird at a peanut feeder.*

series of raw, screeching calls and can be very noisy, especially as they usually move about in small groups.

Jays are commonly found in woodland, wooded parks and large gardens. They take a very wide range of food such as nuts (especially acorns), fruit, insects, and also the eggs and nestlings of other birds. They have a habit of storing food in the autumn, often burying acorns, some of which get forgotten and then germinate, thus helping oak regeneration.

Magpie
Pica pica
Magpies are unmistakable with their bold black-and-white markings and long, graduated tail. They are noisy and sociable birds, often going around in groups and making loud

chattering calls. This already common bird has steadily increased in numbers over recent years. It likes open country with hedges and grassland, woodland margins and also parks and gardens. The nest is large and unusual, being made largely of sticks with a loose domed roof constructed above.

Magpies are often accused of causing songbird declines, but while they do raid other birds' nests to eat eggs and nestlings, there is no evidence that this affects songbird numbers. The magpie enjoys a wide-ranging diet of insects, fruits and seeds, and also scraps.

Jackdaw
Corvus monedula
Jackdaws are small and crow-like, with mainly black

plumage, grey nape and back of head, and a pale eye. They are highly social birds, often nesting in loose colonies around chimneys, cliffs and tall buildings, and in old trees. In winter they frequently form mixed flocks with rooks. Their calls are varied, but mostly strident and cackling. Like magpies, they have become even commoner over the last 20 years, and eat a very wide range of food, including scraps put out in gardens.

Rook
Corvus frugilegus
This familiar member of the crow family is often confused with the carrion crow, but the adults have a pale bill with a bare, pale base, and shaggy 'trousers' at the base of the legs. Rooks nest in colonies, and are noisy and very sociable, making loud and varied raucous calls.

Rooks are widespread and common in lowland areas, preferring open cultivated country and woodland edges, but also suburban areas with trees and parkland or farmland nearby. Rookeries vary in size from just a few to 100 or more pairs, and they tend to stick to traditional sites, ideally in tall trees or woodland adjacent to open fields. They mostly eat grain, but will also take invertebrates such as insect larvae and worms.

Carrion crow
Corvus corone
This all-black crow is about the same size as a rook, but has a black bill and lacks the rook's 'trousers', and nests in solitary pairs rather than in colonies. The call is a monotonous repeated cawing. It is replaced in north and north-west Scotland, and also in Ireland, by the hooded crow, which has a grey body.

Another common bird that has increased in recent years, the carrion crow lives in open country, heathland, light woodland, parks, gardens and urban areas. It will eat almost anything – from seeds, invertebrates, eggs and nestlings, to scraps of all kinds – and is frequently seen foraging in gardens.

Starling
Sturnus vulgaris
Starlings are one of our commonest and most familiar garden birds. They are found almost everywhere, around houses and in woodland and the open countryside. But they have declined markedly in many rural areas, probably as a result of changes in agricultural methods.

Dumpy in shape, and with a rather long, slender bill, starlings are adept at exploiting a wide range of habitats and opportunities. The plumage is a glossy green in spring, becoming spotted white in winter.

Starlings are among the most frequent visitors to gardens. This 'all-purpose' bird can feed on almost anything – insects, worms, scraps, fruit, berries and even insects, caught in circling flight. When feeding on grubs and worms from a lawn, starlings often plunge their beaks into the soil, then open their mandibles to enlarge the hole – a rather different strategy from that of thrushes and blackbirds.

Though not the commonest of visitors to gardens, grey herons (Ardea cinerea) are extremely adept at catching goldfish, which are therefore not recommended for the wildlife garden pond.

A pouch made of natural fibre may entice a pair of robins or other birds to nest, but is also a useful refuge as a roosting site, especially in cold weather.

House sparrow
Passer domesticus

The humble house sparrow needs little introduction. The male has a grey cap and black chin, while the female and young birds are a drab grey-brown. The song is also undistinguished – a rather tuneless chirping.

House sparrows usually nest in loose colonies, building untidy nests. They sometimes use nest boxes, including those intended for blue tits (the sparrows can be excluded by means of a narrow, blue tit-sized entrance hole).

Though widespread in towns and cities, and also in villages and farms, house sparrows have suffered a marked decline in recent years. Though as yet unexplained, it is perhaps due to 'cleaner' farming practices that leave less grain and other food lying around. House sparrows feed on insects in summer and also grain, especially in winter. They are regular at feeders, and take many scraps.

Chaffinch
Fringilla coelebs

Our commonest finch, the chaffinch is a regular and increasingly common visitor to gardens and bird tables. The male in the breeding season has a blue-grey crown, brown back and pinkish breast. The female is olive-brown above and grey-brown below. In flight, chaffinches show a clear white wing patch and bar, and white outer tail feathers. The song is a pleasant, descending cadence, accelerating towards the end, the rhythm of which has been likened to that of a cricket bowler running up to the crease and then delivering the ball with a flourish.

Chaffinches eat mainly insects in spring and summer, but also seeds and berries in autumn and winter.

Bullfinch
Pyrrhula pyrrhula

This large, rather dumpy finch has a clear white rump. The male has bright rose-red underparts, a blue-grey back, and a black head and tail, while the female is a dull brown-grey. The call is a feeble whistle.

Although widespread, the bullfinch has suffered a steep decline since the mid-1970s, possibly because of the loss of trees and hedgerows, or seed-bearing weeds. It is a bird of woodland, scrub, parks and gardens. Apart from seeds and some insects, bullfinches have a great liking for buds, including those of fruit trees. This means they are often attracted to orchards, where they can sometimes be a problem.

Greenfinch
Carduelis chloris
This large yellow-green or brownish finch is seldom absent from gardens. It shows bright-yellow wing and tail patches, especially in flight. The females and young are less brightly coloured, and can look rather sparrow-like. The calls and song contain characteristic wheezy, nasal notes.

Greenfinches eat mainly seeds but also insects, and often visit bird tables and feeders. They are particularly fond of peanuts, and for a large finch are surprisingly agile around hanging nut containers.

Goldfinch
Carduelis carduelis
Surely one of the most attractive of our common garden birds, the goldfinch is a beautifully coloured small finch with black-and-yellow wings and a bright-red face. Goldfinches are usually seen flitting about in flocks, uttering pleasant, tinkling contact flight calls. The song is a rapid sequence of twittering, jingly notes.

Goldfinches are particularly common in lowland areas, especially around hedges, fields, parks, orchards and gardens. Breeding birds tend to migrate south in the winter, replaced to some extent by others from further north. They mainly feed on small seeds such as those of thistles, teasel and other weeds. But they also take insects, and often visit bird feeders, especially where niger seed is available.

Linnet
Carduelis cannabina
This active if somewhat modestly coloured finch is mainly brown, though the male has a red forehead and breast in the breeding season. The linnet has a twittering flight call and quite a musical, rather canary-like song.

Linnets were once much more common, but have declined steadily since the late 1960s, probably because of the reduced availability of weed seeds in agricultural areas.

Heads of teasel that have gone to seed should be left to stand as they may attract visiting goldfinches. These colourful small finches use their narrow bills to extract the tiny seeds from the spiky fruiting heads.

Amphibians and reptiles

Amphibians and reptiles (with the exception of adders) are generally to be encouraged in the wildlife garden. On the whole, amphibians thrive in wet and moist habitats, while reptiles prefer sunny, drier sites – although grass snakes are semi-aquatic (and eat frogs).

Amphibians

To encourage amphibians, the garden pond should have a good balance of open water and areas of dense submerged aquatics such as pondweed *(Elodea)*, water-milfoil *(Myriophyllum)* and hornworts *(Ceratophyllum)*. It should also have swampy margins with emergent plants such as arrowhead *(Sagittaria)*, yellow iris *(Iris pseudacorus)*, bogbean *(Menyanthes trifoliata)* and purple loosestrife *(Lythrum hyssopifolia)*.

Areas of long grass close to the pond are appreciated by frogs, while toads and newts like to be able to hide in damp crevices, such as under logs.

Common frog
Rana temporaria
The frog is our most familiar amphibian (see page 32). It is often found in gardens, especially if there is a pond, stream or marshy area. Frogs have

smooth skin and a rather bony appearance, and can be active and jump well. They lay their eggs (frogspawn) in jelly-like masses, early in the spring.

Common toad
Bufo bufo
Toads have a warty, often dry skin and move less quickly

A toad emerges slowly from underneath a St John's wort (Hypericum) shrub. Although toads breed in water, they spend much of their lives on land, often lurking and hunting in damp, shady sites.

than frogs, and are also less prone to hop or jump. Although they need water to breed, toads are often found in quite dry areas of the garden. Toadspawn is laid in long strings draped around aquatic plants.

Common (smooth) newt
Triturus vulgaris

This is our commonest newt, found throughout most of Europe, Britain and Ireland. It is no more than 10 cm (4 in) long and has a lizard-like appearance (brown above and with a black-spotted orange belly) but its skin is smooth – never scaly and dry like a lizard's.

The common newt breeds in spring, laying 200–300 eggs, which are singly attached to the leaves of aquatic vegetation. During this season, the male develops spectacular crests and colouring, its upper-parts becoming greyer with black spots.

The common newt will eat any invertebrate it can catch, as well as frogspawn and small tadpoles. Being the most terrestrial of the newts, it requires access to suitable earthy habitat as well as a pond.

The male great crested newt is a truly handsome amphibian. In the breeding season it develops a spiky crest along its back and dramatic orange and black colours on its belly.

Palmate newt
Triturus helveticus

The palmate newt tends to prefer more acid ponds than the common newt. It is slightly smaller too, growing only to 9 cm (3.5 in). It is difficult to distinguish from the common newt, but is most easily identified by the lack of spotting on its throat. The hind feet are black and palmate (lobed) – hence the animal's name. The males develop subtle, smooth crests on the tail and a black filament at the end of the tail during the breeding season.

The palmate newt lays up to 460 eggs, which are singly

attached to aquatic vegetation. It feeds on small invertebrates such as earthworms and slugs. When the baby newts emerge onto dry land for the first time, they are easily distinguished by an orange stripe down the middle of the back.

Great crested newt
Triturus cristatus

Adult great crested newts are large, being up to 15 cm (6 in) long, with rough, warty skin that is black above. They have orange-yellow bellies patterned with black, and silvery-white sides. Outside the breeding season, they are likely

to be found under piles of brick or wood, or perhaps under paving stones that are fairly close to water.

The breeding season starts in early spring, when the males develop a spiky crest. The females each lay 200–400 eggs, which they attach singly to aquatic vegetation. These newts eat a variety of invertebrates as well as tadpoles and frogspawn in the water, and will also hunt for slugs at night after rain.

Reptiles

Grass snake
Natrix natrix
This harmless snake is an expert swimmer, and is sometimes found in or around larger garden ponds. Grass snakes feed on live prey including frogs, toads and fish, and can sometimes be seen basking at the water's edge, slithering quickly into the water when disturbed.

The grass snake grows up to 1.2 m (47 in) long – sometimes even longer. The body is generally olive-green in colour with black barring and a bright-yellow collar.

If you handle them, grass snakes hiss and can even feign death. You should also watch out for the pungent, foul-

Grass snakes are not infrequent visitors to larger garden ponds. They are expert swimmers and are particularly fond of feeding on frogs.

smelling liquid which they can eject in self-defence!

You can encourage grass snakes to visit your garden by providing shelter as well as manure heaps that are left undisturbed.

Adder
Vipera berus
The venomous adder is fortunately rare in gardens, but may

occur if your garden adjoins marshy ground or heathland. Adders are generally smaller and plumper than grass snakes and have characteristic bold black zig-zig markings along the back.

Common lizard
Lacerta vivipara
Despite its name, this lizard is not that common, and is not

often seen in gardens. This is partly because it is vulnerable to garden predators such as cats and rats. The common lizard is small, measuring just 17 cm (6.5 in) long, and its tail accounts for half its full length. It is brown, often with an olive iridescence and an orange or reddish underside.

Common lizards retain their eggs within their bodies and give birth to tiny, jet-black, fully-formed baby lizards that are well adapted for heat absorption. They will eat almost any small invertebrate, and also some fruit such as blackberries in autumn.

To attract common lizards, you need to have a garden that is cat-free and (ideally) south-facing, and it also needs to be

equipped with embankments (for basking in the sun) and piles of brush or stones (to provide cover).

Slow worm
Anguis fragilis

A lizard without legs, resembling a small snake or huge worm, the slow worm has very fine scales and is shiny and smooth. It is generally bronze or pinkish in colour. The females may have dark undersides and some have blue spotting on the sides.

Because of its resemblance to snakes, this animal has sadly been needlessly persecuted. It is not uncommon in gardens, especially in the south and west. It is, however, more likely to be found in rural

Slow worms tend to be found on warm, dry banks and hedges, especially in the south-west of Britain. Smooth and rather featureless, they are often a coppery colour.

gardens or in churchyards, and its presence can be encouraged with log and stone piles in the garden, which it may use for basking and shelter.

Slow worms feed on small slugs, earthworms and other soft-bodied invertebrates. During the breeding season they retain 6–12 eggs within the body, laying them at the point of hatching. Young slow worms are bright coppery above and jet-black below, with a thin black line running down the back.

Insects and other invertebrates

Insects and a host of other invertebrates are the garden's (mostly) unseen toilers and helpers, and only a small minority of them cause damage to garden plants. They are an essential part of the wildlife garden ecosystem, and we should do all we can to encourage most of them.

Butterflies and moths
Lepidoptera

Common garden butterflies

Brimstone
Gonepteryx rhamni
Large and bright yellow (male) or creamy greenish-white (female), these familiar butter-flies appear early in the year after hibernating. The larvae feed on buckthorn or alder buckthorn, and fresh adults emerge in the summer. The adults are particularly keen on thistle flowers.

Large white
Pieris brassicae
This familiar species is disliked by most gardeners as the caterpillars attack brassicas and also nasturtiums, often with devastating results. But it does not usually appear in large enough numbers to do huge

damage in the garden, espe-cially if the plants are well mixed. It is a large butterfly with black spots and wing tips.

Small white
Pieris rapae
Like a small, more delicate version of large white, this species is less damaging in the garden, partly because the eggs are laid singly. Brassicas, nasturtiums and wild crucifers are the larval food plants, while the adults feed from a wide range of flowers.

Green-veined white
Pieris napi
Very similar to the small white, this pretty butterfly has much more obvious veins, especially on the underside. It is not a garden pest as it lays its eggs mostly on wild crucifers such as garlic mustard and charlock. Lavender is a favourite food for the adults.

The bright-blue flowers of bugle (Ajuga reptans) are highly attrac-tive to many insects, notably bees and butterflies.

Plants for butterflies (including larval food plants and adult nectar sources)

Agrimony	*Agrimonia eupatorium*	Mallow	*Malva* species
Alder buckthorn	*Frangula alnus*	Marjoram	*Origanum officinale*
Aubretia	*Aubrieta deltoidea*	Meadow cranesbill	*Geranium pratense*
Bird's foot trefoil	*Lotus corniculatus*	Michaelmas daisy	*Aster novi-belgii*
Blackthorn	*Prunus spinosa*	Mignonette	*Reseda odorata*
Bramble	*Rubus* species	Mint	*Mentha* species
Broom	*Cytisus scoparius*	Nettle	*Urtica dioica, U. urens*
Buckthorn	*Rhamnus catharticus*	Oak	*Quercus robur, Q. petraea*
Buddleia	*Buddleia davidii*	Ox-eye daisy	*Leucanthemum vulgare*
Bugle	*Ajuga reptans*	Perennial flax	*Linum anglicum*
Catmint	*Nepeta cataria*	Primrose	*Primula vulgaris*
Charlock	*Sinapis arvensis*	Privet	*Ligustrum vulgare*
Common knapweed	*Centaurea nigra*	Purple loosestrife	*Lythrum salicaria*
Corn marigold	*Chrysanthemum segetum*	Ragged robin	*Lychnis flos-cuculi*
Cornflower	*Centaurea cyanus*	Red hot poker	*Kniphofia* species
Cowslip	*Primula veris*	Red valerian	*Centranthus ruber*
Cuckooflower	*Cardamine pratensis*	Restharrow	*Ononis repens*
Dog violet	*Viola riviniana*	Rock rose	*Helianthemum* species
Fennel	*Foeniculum vulgare*	Rosemary	*Rosmarinus officinalis*
Field scabious	*Knautia arvensis*	Rowan	*Sorbus aucuparia*
Forget-me-not	*Myosotis arvensis*	Sage	*Salvia* species
Foxglove	*Digitalis purpurea*	St John's wort	*Hypericum* species
Garlic mustard	*Alliaria petiolata*	Sea holly	*Eryngium maritimum*
Germander	*Veronica chamaedrys*	Selfheal	*Prunella vulgaris*
speedwell		Small scabious	*Scabiosa columbaria*
Globe-thistle	*Echinops sphaerocephalus*	Soapwort	*Saponaria officinalis*
Goldenrod	*Solidago canadensis,*	Sweet rocket	*Hesperis matronalis*
	S. virgaurea	Sweet scabious	*Scabiosa atropurpurea*
Greater knapweed	*Centaurea scabiosa*	Sweet violet	*Viola odorata*
Greater stitchwort	*Stellaria holostea*	Sweet William	*Dianthus barbatus*
Guelder rose	*Viburnum opulus*	Teasel	*Dipsacus fullonum*
Hawthorn	*Crataegus monogyna*	Thistle	*Cirsium* species,
Hedge mustard	*Sisymbrium officinale*		*Carduus* species
Helenium	*Helenium autumnale*	Thrift	*Armeria maritima*
Holly	*Ilex aquifolium*	Thyme	*Thymus* species
Hollyhock	*Alcea rosea*	Toadflax	*Linaria vulgaris*
Honesty	*Lunaria annua*	Vervain	*Verbena officinalis*
Hop	*Humulus lupulus*	Viper's bugloss	*Echium vulgare*
Hyssop	*Hyssopus officinalis*	Wallflower	*Cheiranthus cheiri*
Ice plant	*Sedum spectabile*	Weld	*Reseda luteola*
Ivy	*Hedera helix*	Wild strawberry	*Fragaria vesca*
Kidney vetch	*Anthyllis vulneraria*	Winter savory	*Satureia montana*
Lavender	*Lavandula angustifolia*	Yellow alyssum	*Alyssum saxatile*

Orange tip
Anthocaris cardamines

The female can be confused with one of the small whites (although the underside of the hind wing is marbled), but the male is distinctive, with bright-orange wingtips. This species has increased in numbers, and may often be seen in gardens. It is on the wing from April to early July. The caterpillars eat crucifers, and also honesty in the garden.

Common blue
Polyommatus icarus

This butterfly is often seen in larger gardens, especially those with wild, grassy areas. The male is bright blue above, the female mainly brown with marginal orange spots. The larvae eat bird's-foot trefoil and clovers. It is mainly on the wing from May to September.

Holly blue
Celastrina argiolus

This active butterfly is now quite common in gardens, especially around holly trees or ivy, which are the larval food plants of the first and second broods respectively. It is not found in Scotland, although its range is steadily expanding northwards. Both male and female are blue above, the female with black wingtips; the underside is pale with tiny black speckles.

Red admiral
Vanessa atalanta

Among our largest and prettiest species, red admirals appear as migrants, mostly in late May or June, although some of them hibernate and emerge earlier.

The caterpillar's favourite food plant is the nettle, and the adults visit many flowers, notably sedums, Michaelmas daisies and buddleias.

Painted lady
Vanessa cardui

Another migrant species, whose numbers vary from year to year, the painted lady lays its eggs mainly on thistles, though sometimes on nettles or mallows. This butterfly is a strong flier and has an attractive orange, black and white chequered wing pattern.

Small tortoiseshell
Aglais urticae

This is one of the commonest garden species, and also one of the earliest to emerge from hibernation – usually in March. The adults can be seen throughout most of the year. Nettles are the favoured larval food and the caterpillars spin untidy webs.

Peacock
Inachis io

Although dark, almost black beneath, when the peacock opens its wings, it reveals bright eye-spots to deter predators (see page 21).

The adults can live for nearly a year, and hibernate in hollow trees, garden sheds and the like. They emerge early in spring, with a new generation in July. They love many nectar-rich flowers, such as buddleias, thistles, knapweed and teasel.

Red admirals sometimes feed on fruits such as rotting apples in the autumn, or as here on a plum.

Comma
Polygonia c-album

The name comes from the comma-shaped white spot on the underside of the hind wing. Above, this species is bright orange with black blotches, but the most unusual feature is the ragged outline of the wings. This is another butterfly that lays its eggs on nettles, but also on hops. The adults emerge early after hibernating.

Below Numbers of painted lady, a migrant species, vary from year to year. This beautiful butterfly is here seen feeding in the autumn on an ice plant (Sedum).

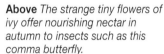

Above The strange tiny flowers of ivy offer nourishing nectar in autumn to insects such as this comma butterfly.

Speckled wood
Pararge aegeria

The speckled, dusky plumage of this delightful butterfly chimes well with its favoured habitat – the dappled sunlight of open woodland glades – but it is increasingly found in gardens as well. The eggs are laid on various grass species, and both caterpillars and chrysalises may overwinter.

Less-common garden butterflies

Wall
Lasiommata megera

This increasingly rare butterfly is orange-brown in colour, delicately patterned with dark

A gatekeeper butterfly feeds on wild marjoram (Origanum vulgare). *This pretty butterfly has a short flight season – from late June until early September. It is found mainly along sunny hedges and lanes, but also in wilder gardens, especially where there are brambles and long grass.*

brown. The larvae eat various grasses, including Yorkshire fog, false brome, cock's-foot and annual meadow-grass. The wall butterfly is aptly named after its habit of basking on walls and rocky areas. Though occasionally seen in some suitable gardens, it prefers open grassland where the turf is broken or stony. It can also be found in coastal habitats, as well as in quarries and along railway embankments.

Gatekeeper
Pyronia tithonus
The gatekeeper prefers open woodland, grassland and hedgerows, and is particularly fond of bramble *(Rubus)* flowers. It is light brown with large orange-brown patches on its wings and one eye-spot on each forewing. The female is slightly paler. This charming butterfly is quite commonly seen in gardens adjacent to fields or woodland.

Meadow brown
Maniola jurtina
As its name implies, the meadow brown is found mainly in grassy, open spaces, but also in woodlands and along forest edges. It does, however, sometimes venture into grassy gardens.

The adult butterfly is well camouflaged, being dark brown with an eye-spot on each forewing and pale brown on the underside. The female is marked with orange-brown.

Ringlet
Aphantopus hyperantus
The ringlet prefers open woodland, hedgerows and damp meadows, but is sometimes found in wilder gardens, especially if there is plenty of bramble *(Rubus)*. It is dark brown with one or two eye-like markings on each wing. The underside is dark brown with several yellow-ringed black eye-spots.

Large skipper
Ochlodes venatus
This butterfly favours grassy hillsides, forest edges and roadsides, but it sometimes turns up in grassy gardens. It is orange-brown with some darker markings on the forewings. It pupates within a cocoon amongst grass blades.

Small copper
Lycaena phlaeas
This small firebrand is a fast, aggressive butterfly with bright shiny orange forewings. Though most abundant on heathland, where the larvae feed on sorrel, it may be especially common in hot summers, when it sometimes strays into gardens.

Commoner garden moths
We have included here just a small selection of the many moths that are commonly found in gardens. For further information you should consult a more detailed identification guide.

Hawkmoths
Hawkmoths are some of the largest moths, and many of them have triangular-shaped

Plants for moths (including larval food plants and adult nectar sources)

Angelica	*Angelica archangelica*	Marjoram	*Origanum officinale*
Barberry	*Berberis vulgaris*	Meadow clary	*Salvia pratensis*
Birch	*Betula* species	Meadowsweet	*Filipendula ulmaria*
Blackthorn	*Prunus spinosa*	Mullein	*Verbascum* species
Bramble	*Rubus* species	Nettle	*Urtica dioica, U. urens*
Centaury	*Centaurium* species	Oak	*Quercus robur,*
Common knapweed	*Centaurea nigra*		*Q. petraea*
Cowslip	*Primula veris*	Ox-eye daisy	*Leucanthemum vulgare*
Dandelion	*Taraxacum officinale*	Plantain	*Plantago* species
Dock	*Rumex* species	Poplar (and aspen)	*Populus* species
Evening primrose	*Oenothera* species	Primrose	*Primula vulgaris*
Foxglove	*Digitalis purpurea*	Purple loosestrife	*Lythrum salicaria*
Goldenrod	*Solidago canadensis,*	Ragged robin	*Lychnis flos-cuculi*
	S. virgaurea	Red campion	*Silene dioica*
Harebell	*Campanula rotundifolia*	Red clover	*Trifolium pratense*
Hawthorn	*Crataegus monogyna,*	Red valerian	*Centranthus ruber*
	C. laevigata	Rock rose	*Helianthemum* species
Heather	*Calluna vulgaris*	Sea kale	*Crambe maritima*
Hedge woundwort	*Stachys sylvatica*	Sweet rocket	*Hesperis matronalis*
Herb Bennet	*Geum urbanum*	Toadflax	*Linaria* species
(wood avens)		Tobacco	*Nicotiana* species
Herb Robert	*Geranium robertianum*	Traveller's joy	*Clematis vitalba*
Honeysuckle	*Lonicera periclymenum*	Viper's bugloss	*Echium vulgare*
Lady's bedstraw	*Galium verum*	White campion	*Silene alba*
Lemon balm	*Melissa officinalis*	Wild pansy	*Viola tricolor*
Lime	*Tilia* species	Willow	*Salix* species
Maiden pink	*Dianthus deltoides*	Yarrow	*Achillea millefolium*

wings. They fly mostly at night and can often be found around exterior lights.

Broad-bordered bee hawkmoth
Hemaris fuciformis
This species has transparent, bee-like wings spanning 4–5 cm (1.5–2 in), and is a day-flying summer visitor, mainly to southern counties. It hovers at nectar-rich flowers and flies more quickly than the bumble-bees it resembles.

Eyed hawkmoth
Smerinthus ocellata
These beautiful hawkmoths have marbled brown forewings and pink hindwings that have a central large blue-and-black eye-spot. The caterpillars are pale yellow-green with white or red-centred spots on the side, pale diagonal stripes and a green tail horn. They pupate in September in a cocoon just below the surface of the ground. The caterpillars feed on willow, poplar and apple.

Hummingbird hawkmoth
Macroglossum stellatarum
The hummingbird hawkmoth is another day-flying moth – a summer visitor from further south in Europe. As its name suggests, it has a very fast flight resembling that of a humming-bird, and can be found hover-ing in front of highly scented flowers such as jasmine.

Privet hawkmoth
Sphinx ligustri

One of the commonest garden hawkmoths. The caterpillars are bright green with seven purplish-red and white diagonal stripes, and grow to about 10 cm (4 in) long. They feed on lilac and ash as well as privet. The adult has brown forewings, streaked black, and the hindwings have pink and black banding. The abdomen is also striped pink and black.

Other moths
Brimstone moth
Opisthograptis luteolata

Bright yellow and fairly large, this moth is frequent in gardens, and is on the wing from spring through to late summer. The larvae feed on many plants, including blackthorn and hawthorn.

Lime hawkmoth
Mimas tiliae

If you have lime trees nearby, you may be lucky enough to spot this pretty hawkmoth, which has pale-brown wings patterned with green-brown patches. The caterpillars feed on lime, alder and elm, but the adults do not feed.

Poplar hawkmoth
Laothoe populi

The wings of the adult are shades of grey and have a scalloped margin; the hindwings are red-brown near to the body. The caterpillars feed on poplar and willow, but the adults do not feed.

The silver Y is one of our commoner moths. Here it is feeding on a lily at night, with its proboscis extended to obtain nectar from inside the flower.

Broad-bordered yellow underwing
Noctua fimbriata

At rest this fairly large moth is well camouflaged, but during flight its brightly coloured black-and-orange hindwings are exposed. It often appears in gardens, where it is attracted to exterior lights. The caterpillars feed on a range of plants including hawthorn, bramble, dock, primrose and deadnettle.

Cinnabar moth
Tyria jacobaeae

The cinnabar is a shy, mainly night-flying moth whose spectacular appearance acts as a warning to predators of its distastefulness. It has a black body, black-and-red wings with two red wing spots, and a wingspan of 3.5–4.5 cm (1.4–1.8 in).

The caterpillars have a warning colouration of bright-yellow and black bands to discourage predators; they grow to 3 cm (1.2 in) and feed most commonly on ragwort.

Garden tiger
Arctia caja
This attractive moth has brown-and-white forewings and bright-orange hindwings with navy blue/black spots. The caterpillars feed on a wide range of wild and garden plants, including dandelion and nettle. Pupation occurs within a white silk cocoon.

Magpie moth
Abraxas grossulariata
This pretty moth has black blotches on a cream-and-orange background, and is often seen flying during the day. The caterpillar's main food plants are blackthorn, hawthorn and currants.

Pussmoth
Cerura vinula
The adult pussmoth has a wingspan of 2.5 cm (1 in) and is white with black markings and feathery antennae – its furry appearance accounts for its name!

The caterpillar is spectacular, growing up to 6.5 cm (2.5 in) long. It is very plump and bright green, with a red 'face' and a tapering tail that ends in two long filaments. It turns plum-coloured before pupating and makes a hard cocoon on the bark of a tree.

Purple loosestrife makes a splendidly colourful addition to the wildlife garden. It grows best in damp soil around ponds and alongside streams, and its long flowerheads attract many pollinating insects.

Silver Y
Autographa gamma
One of our commoner moths, migrating north each year from southern Europe, the silver Y often flies by day as well as at night. It is named for the inverted Y shape on its grey-brown forewings.

Dragonflies and damselflies
Odonata
About 40 species of dragonflies and damselflies occur in Britain, and of these about a dozen may be spotted in gardens, especially if you have a medium-sized or large pond.

In addition to being attractive insects, both larvae and adults eat other insects, including midges and mosquitoes.

Damselflies
Zygoptera
Damselflies are slender, have a weak, fluttery flight, and when at rest hold their wings closed over the abdomen.

Azure damselfly
Coenagrion puella
This common species often breeds in garden ponds, flying between mid-May and late August. Males and some females are blue with black rings, while some females have a green background.

Blue-tailed damselfly
Ischnura elegans
One of the commonest species, this damselfly usually has a dark, shiny body with an obvious blue band towards the tip. It is remarkably adaptable and is an early coloniser of new ponds, tolerating a degree of pollution.

Common blue damselfly
Enallagma cyathigerum
One of the commonest species, it is often abundant and may colonise a garden pond. The flight season is from May to early September. It is bright blue with black rings and a club-shaped mark on segment 2. It prefers ponds with large areas of open water. The larvae lurk amongst pondweeds.

Dragonflies
Anisoptera
Dragonflies have more robust bodies, are strong and powerful in flight and hold their wings open when at rest.

Broad-bodied chaser
Libellula depressa
This bulky dragonfly has a broad, flat abdomen, which is pale blue in mature males and yellow/brown in females and immature males with pale yellow lateral spots.

This insect quickly colonises new sites, including garden ponds, and spends long periods perched on vegetation in between flights, which are speedy and direct.

Four-spotted chaser
Libella quadrimaculata
Both sexes of this species have a tapering dark-brown abdomen with yellow sides and a black tip. The wings are marked with striking brown patches. It is usually seen perched on vegetation at the water's edge around pools, ditches and garden ponds. The territorial flight is characteristically aggressive.

Common darter
Sympetrum striolatum
This small, restless dragonfly occurs in a range of habitats, from lakes and rivers to ditches and garden ponds. The abdomen is reddish orange in the male and yellow/brown in the female and immature male, though older females turn reddish.

Brown hawker
Aeshna grandis
The brown hawker is a large brown dragonfly whose beautiful wings are suffused with amber. Appearing in mid to late summer, it will breed in garden ponds but also strays quite far from water. It has a characteristic gliding and looping flight interspersed with shallow wing beats.

The broad-bodied chaser (Libellula depressa) rapidly colonises large garden ponds and may often be spotted sunning itself on waterside vegetation.

A hawker dragonfly (Aeshna species) emerges from its larval exoskeleton. At this stage the adult is rather vulnerable as it must then pump up its wings before it is able to fly.

Common hawker
Aeshna juncea

The common hawker breeds in a variety of still waters, including garden ponds. The male has blue spots on a blackish background, and the female yellow spots on a brown background. The adults are fast and powerful in flight. Larval development takes 3–4 years, but the larvae soon acquire a characteristic striped appearance.

Migrant hawker
Aeshna mixta

Male migrant hawkers are predominantly blue; females are a dull greenish yellow or

A hawker dragonfly (Aeshna species) emerges from its larval exoskeleton. At this stage the adult is rather vulnerable as it must then pump up its wings before it is able to fly.

brown. They can be seen flying high around treetops, in open woodland and meadows, sometimes soaring to a great height after prey, mainly in late summer and autumn. The larvae are found in ponds as well as lakes, gravel pits and slow-moving canals and rivers. This species is found mainly in southern counties.

Southern hawker
Aeshna cyanea

In flight the southern hawker holds its body horizontally and the abdomen has a slight curve. It tends to be seen flying alone. Males have bright-green markings that become blue

towards the tip of the abdomen; females are stouter and are patterned yellow and green. Southern hawkers are often found in and around garden ponds, and may be attracted into gardens that resemble woodland clearings.

Emperor
Anax imperator

This impressive dragonfly has a vigorous agility in flight that is unrivalled among British species. On a summer's day the male can be admired hovering and circumnavigating a pond from a height of several metres. The male has a green thorax and a blue down-curved abdomen with black linear markings along the dorsal surface. The females are predominantly green, although they may turn blue in warm weather. It lives mainly in southern Britain.

A southern hawker dragonfly rests on a water lily flower. This is another dragonfly that may colonise the garden pond.

Common wasps gain their nourishment from many sources – for example, smaller insects, scraps, fruit and jam – but they also sip nectar from flowers, including those of ivy.

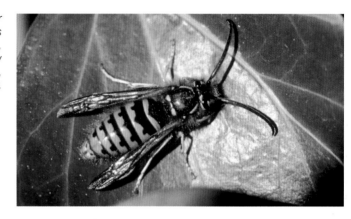

Plants for bees (nectar sources)

Agrimony	*Agrimonia eupatorium*	Lovage	*Levisticum officinale*
Angelica	*Angelica archangelica*	Marjoram	*Origanum officinale*
Bergamot	*Monarda didyma*	Meadow clary	*Salvia pratensis*
Bird's foot trefoil	*Lotus corniculatus*	Meadowsweet	*Filipendula ulmaria*
Black horehound	*Ballota nigra*	Mint	*Mentha* species
Blackthorn	*Prunus spinosa*	Mullein	*Verbascum* species
Borage	*Borago officinalis*	Musk mallow	*Malva moschata*
Bugle	*Ajuga reptans*	Penstemon	*Penstemon* species
Cardoon	*Cynara cardunculus*	Purple loosestrife	*Lythrum salicaria*
Catmint	*Nepeta cataria*	Ragged robin	*Lychnis flos-cuculi*
Chicory	*Cichorium intybus*	Red clover	*Trifolium pratense*
Chives	*Allium schoenoprasum*	Red deadnettle	*Lamium purpureum*
Columbine	*Aquilegia vulgaris*	Red valerian	*Centranthus ruber*
Cuckooflower	*Cardamine pratensis*	Rock rose	*Helianthemum* species
Foxglove	*Digitalis purpurea*	Rosemary	*Rosmarinus officinalis*
Germander speedwell	*Veronica chamaedrys*	Sage	*Salvia* species
		Sainfoin	*Onobrychis viciifolia*
Globe thistle	*Echinops sphaerocephalus*	Selfheal	*Prunella vulgaris*
Globeflower	*Trollius europaeus*	Spiked speedwell	*Veronica spicata*
Greater knapweed	*Centaurea scabiosa*	Sweet William	*Dianthus barbatus*
Hedge woundwort	*Stachys sylvatica*	Thyme	*Thymus* species
Herb Robert	*Geranium robertianum*	Toadflax	*Linaria vulgaris*
Hollyhock	*Alcea rosea*	Viper's bugloss	*Echium vulgare*
Hyssop	*Hyssopus officinalis*	White deadnettle	*Lamium album*
Lamb's ears	*Stachys byzantina*	Wild basil	*Clinopodium vulgare*
Lavender	*Lavandula angustifolia*	Yellow flag iris	*Iris pseudacorus*
Lemon balm	*Melissa officinalis*	Yellow loosestrife	*Lysimachia vulgaris*

A buff-tailed bumblebee (Bombus terrestris) *feeds on a knapweed flower* (Centaurea nigra). *In the process it becomes covered with pollen, which it may then transfer to another flower.*

Bees and wasps

There are over 120,000 species of Hymenoptera ('membrane-winged' insects) worldwide, varying greatly in size, shape, breeding biology and general behaviour. The most familiar of these in the garden are bees, wasps and ants, most of which are beneficial, forming an important part of the garden ecosystem and helping to pollinate flowers. The following are some of the commonest species of bee and wasp:

Common wasp
Vespula vulgaris

This is the most common and widespread species of wasp. It has a characteristic black-and-yellow abdomen and is 1.5 cm (0.5 in) long. Its nests of papery chewed wood are often built in tree hollows or in outbuildings or attics. Wasps are important predators in the garden ecosystem.

Honey bee
Apis mellifera

The common honey bee is an important pollinator of fruit trees and other crops, and also garden flowers. The worker bees feed on nectar and pollen, and make honey as a stored food supply.

This bee is a rather non-descript brown colour and can sometimes be found swarming in hollow trees and roofs. Colonies, which are normally in hives, consist of about 50,000 workers with one egg-laying queen.

Bumblebees
Bombus species

Six species of bumblebee are commonly seen in gardens in Britain. They are important pollinators and should be welcomed in the wildlife garden. Bumblebees can be encouraged by planting flowers belonging to the mint family such as deadnettle, mint, sage or lavender.

The queens emerge from hibernation early in spring, at which time they enjoy flowers such as white deadnettle and flowering currant. After feeding up, they start to look for a place to found a nest colony, which usually consists of about 50 to 150 individuals.

You can provide suitable nest sites such as log-piles or the purpose-built bee nest boxes that can be purchased from garden centres and various suppliers (see overleaf). Such boxes can be baited with cotton (use upholsterer's cotton, not cotton wool, as the latter can get entangled in the bees' delicate feet).

Buff-tailed bumblebee
B. terrestris

This large bumblebee is black, with a yellow collar and a yellow band on the abdomen; the worker has a white tip to the tail, while the queen has a yellow or buff tail tip. This bee is common in gardens and nests in the soil. It is the biggest species to be found frequently in gardens – the queen is always over 2 cm (0.8 in) long, with a wingspan of up to 43 mm. It is also one of the earliest bees to appear: in mild winters, the first can be seen flying about in February, and individuals may still be on the wing until mid-October.

Common carder-bee
B. pascuorum

This very common bumblebee emerges in early spring, nesting on the surface in small colonies (usually 80–100). Adults can be seen late in the year – even into November. It is one of the smaller species and has a reddish-brown tail. The entire thorax is covered in brownish-yellow hairs (where-

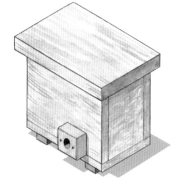

Suitable nesting boxes for bumblebees (above) and solitary mason bees (Osmia species; right).

as most species show a band of black hairs as well).

The common carder-bee has adapted iself to human presence and hardly ever stings. Although it lives in woodland, it also breeds in parks (even those in big cities) and gardens.

Early bumblebee
B. pratorum

This is a small species that nests early in the year, and is common in gardens. The workers and the males are just a tiny bit smaller than those of the common carder-bee. The front part of the thorax is covered with bright-yellow hairs, and may be entirely covered, especially in males. Often the first part of the abdomen is yellow as well, and the tail is strikingly orange. In

The large, showy flowers of the foxglove are much visited by bumblebees.

older specimens the colouring may be less striking, as the hairs tend to become dirty white as in many other species, making them harder to identify.

Garden bumblebee
B. hortorum

This relatively large bumblebee has a furry abdomen and thorax. The thorax is black and yellow, the abdomen black and white/grey. It usually nests below ground – for example, in a mouse or vole hole. It is particularly common in sunny, south-facing gardens.

Red-tailed bumblebee
B. lapidarius

This bee is very common in the south, emerging in early spring and usually nesting underground, often in large colonies.

This distinctive species is mostly black except for its red tail. In the vicinity of the nest it is more aggressive than most

Adult hoverflies are attractive insects that mimic bees and wasps, and the larvae of some are voracious predators of aphids. So they should always be welcomed into a wildlife garden.

colouring, however, is brighter in this species than in the similar garden bumblebee. In spring it frequents fruit trees and in summer it readily visits many cultivated garden flowers.

Hoverflies
Family Syrphidae
There are about 250 species of hoverfly in Britain, and several are common in gardens. Hoverflies have evolved to resemble harmful wasps, but they are nonetheless true flies, and stingless. They are incredibly mobile in flight, hovering, then darting quickly to a new position – their behaviour is quite different from that of a wasp.

Gardeners should encourage hoverflies, as the larvae of many species eat aphids and other harmful insects, and the adults are important pollinators. The adults are often attracted to the flat flower-heads of umbellifers (members of the carrot family) such as fennel and hogweed.

Grasshoppers and crickets
Orthoptera
Grasshoppers and crickets are sometimes seen in gardens – especially in larger gardens with extensive areas of meadow-height grass. Here are just two of the commoner species we might expect to encounter:

Common field grasshopper
Chorthippus brunneus
This lively insect may be found in grassy gardens, especially on meadow-like sites where the grasses have been allowed to grow tall and mature.

other species of bumblebee, and the queens are large.

The red-tailed bumblebee adapts easily to man-made changes in the natural environment, and will even adopt small flowerbeds in the middle of big cities, as well as parks and gardens. It feeds on over 200 species of flowers, including many exotic garden plants.

White-tailed bumblebee
B. lucorum
This species is black, with one yellow band on the thorax just behind the head, another yellow band on the abdomen, and a white tail. The yellow

The common field grasshopper (Chorthippus brunneus) is quite frequent in gardens in areas where the grass has been allowed to grow to its natural height.

The seven-spot ladybird (Coccinella 7-punctata) *is one of the commonest of our garden ladybirds. It also consumes large numbers of aphids.*

Beetles
Coleoptera

There are more than 4,000 species of beetle in Britain, and several are common in gardens, where most do no harm at all.

Ladybirds
Family Coccinellidae

These familiar garden friends are brightly coloured beetles, their bright colours being a signal to predators that they taste nasty and are not worth eating. As any gardener will tell you, ladybirds perform an essential service by consuming large quantities of aphids.

Ground beetles
Family Carabidae

Ground beetles are mainly black and shiny, and are highly active, chasing and catching smaller invertebrates in the soil and leaf litter.

Stag beetles
Family Lucanidae

Stag beetle
Lucanus cervus

Britain's largest beetle, the stag beetle is some-times seen in gardens in southern England, but it has declined in recent years. The larvae feed in dead wood and it does no harm in the garden. Nor is it dangerous, even though the male has fearful-looking jaws.

Lesser stag beetle
Dorcus parallelopipedus

This is like a smaller version of the stag beetle, and rather commoner.

These grasshoppers jump well, using their powerful hind legs, and are most active in midsummer and autumn. They cause no damage to garden flowers, feeding mainly on grasses, which they chew using their tough mandibles.

Oak bush cricket
Meconema thalassinum

This cricket is a delicate and attractive insect with long antennae, long legs and, in the case of the female, a long, curved ovipositor. It is bright pale green with a darker stripe along the back.

If you have trees and shrubs in or near your garden, you may be lucky enough to spot one of these insects, especially in the autumn, when they may be attracted to lights. They feed mainly on oak or lime trees.

The male stag beetle (Lucanus cervus) *is an impressive insect, and Britain's largest. Like a stag's antlers these oversized mandibles are used mainly in male–male ritual jousting.*

Devil's coach-horse
Staphylinus olens
This common garden beetle is flightless and has a long, flexible body that it arches up when disturbed. It comes out at night to feed on slugs and other small invertebrates, and is often found hiding underneath logs or around compost heaps.

Sexton beetles
Family Silphidae
These beetles are so named because of the important role they play in burying and consuming dead animals, recycling the breakdown products into the soil.

Cockchafer
Melolontha melolontha
Adult cockchafers (or maybugs) have a buzzing, bumbling flight and often collide with windows. The adults are harmless but the larvae, known as rookworms, damage the roots of grasses and can be a nuisance.

Vine weevil
Otiorhynchus sulcatus
Although most weevils are harmless, this species causes damage to a range of garden plants. The adults eat semi-circular pieces out of the leaves of a range of species, including rhododendrons, camellias and fuchsias. The larvae feed on various plant roots, often killing the plant.

Earwigs
Dermaptera
Earwigs are long, brownish insects, either wingless or with short wings that are normally tucked away and invisible. They have curved, pincer-like cerci at the tip of their bodies, but

The common garden centipede Lithobius forficatus *plays a useful role in the garden by eating harmlul pests, and does no damage to garden plants.*

are in fact harmless. They are active by night, resting up during the day in hollow stems and the like. They are helpful in the garden, feeding on aphids, other small insects (dead and alive) and some plant material.

Of the four species of earwig native to Britain, the commonest in gardens is *Forficula auricularia*.

Woodlice

Woodlice are crustaceans, related to crabs and shrimps, but they live on the land, unlike most members of this group. However, they are mostly restricted to wet or damp sites.

There are about 35 species in Britain, of which about half a dozen are common in gardens. Amongst the most frequent are *Oniscus asellus, Porcellio scaber, Philoscia muscorum, Trichoniscus pusillus* and *Armadillidium vulgare* (pill woodlouse). *Armadillidium* species (pill bugs) can roll up into a ball to help conserve moisture and for protection. One species, *Platyarthrus hoffmanseggii*, is tiny, white and blind, and lives inside ants' nests.

Woodlice play a major role in breaking down waste and enriching the soil.

Centipedes and millipedes

Centipedes have a single pair of legs on each body segment, while millipedes have two pairs per segment. Another difference is that centipedes have flattened bodies, while millipedes are more rounded in cross-section. Centipedes have between 15 and 70 pairs of legs (depending on the species), whereas most millipedes have more; there are some millipede species with over 200 pairs.

Lithobius forficatus is a common garden centipede. It has an orange body and powerful jaws, and is a useful garden predator.

Spiders

There are over 600 species of spider in Britain, and they may be found in a wide range of habitats.

Garden spider
Araneus diadematus
One of the commonest of the larger garden species, the garden spider creates the familiar round webs (see picture on page 78), and can often be spotted waiting at the centre of the web, ready to run along the threads to capture flying insects that blunder into the trap. Victims, which may include active, venomous insects such as wasps, are quickly wrapped in a shroud of sticky silk and subdued with a poisonous bite, to be consumed at leisure.

Zebra spider
Salticus scenicus
The zebra spider is usually found on walls or fences, and sometimes inside the house, normally near a window. Small and active, with a stripy black-

nd-white pattern, this spider s a hunter, catching its prey by talking and jumping.

Woodlouse-eating spider
Dysdera crocata
This very unusual garden spider is often found in dark, damp sites. It has an orange body, a pale abdomen and large fangs with which it catches woodlice during nocturnal hunting forays.

Earthworms
Earthworms do a great recycling job in the garden and play a major role in creating fertile soil. They feed mainly on leaves and other decaying plant matter, which they drag undergound before digesting it. One of the commonest garden species is *Lumbricus terrestris*, which grows up to about 25cm (10 in) long.

Earthworms can sometimes be spotted on damp nights at the surface, where the hermaphrodite adults meet to mate. As well as their important recycling role, earthworms are food for many garden birds, and also for some mammals, notably badgers.

Snails and slugs
Of the 20 or so species of slugs and snails that are found in British gardens, there are only two or three which cause serious damage to garden plants and vegetables, the worst being small grey slugs and garden snails.

The garden snail *(Helix aspersa)* is the commonest and largest of the garden snails. Even though it munches through many plants, it is not usually a serious problem except in small gardens in

chalk or limestone areas, or in gardens bounded by old walls with lime-rich mortar. It needs the calcium for healthy shell-building.

Another common garden snail is the white-lipped banded snail *(Cepaea hortensis)*, which is smaller than the garden snail and has a pretty shell, variably patterned with stripes that follow the spiral. It does far less damage than the garden snail.

Regular culling is probably the best way to keep down snail numbers. One should also encourage natural predators such as hedgehogs, thrushes, toads and beetles. Biological control using tiny parasitic nematodes (roundworms) is also possible, and these can be purchased from garden suppliers.

Physical methods of keeping these animals away from vulnerable plants include mulching with bark, or surrounding them with grit, pine needles or ash. In dry weather you could try watering your plants in the early morning rather than late in the evening, because snails come out at night, especially in damp conditions.

Garden snails (Helix aspersa) *are most active at night, especially in wet weather. When they occur in large numbers, they can cause considerable damage to vulnerable plants such as sweet peas and morning glories.*

Useful information

We are often unaware of just how many spiders there are until the dew or frost picks out their decorative webs. Here hoar frost has created a work of art from a web in a gorse bush.

Organisations

The Wildlife Trusts (WT)
The Kiln
Waterside
Mather Road
Newark
Nottinghamshire
NG24 1WT
Tel. 0870 0367711

This partnership of 47 local Wildlife Trusts is the largest UK charity exclusively dedicated to conserving all our habitats and species. It has a membership of more than 530,000.

More than 2,500 sites in the UK are cared for as nature reserves by the Wildlife Trusts. Together, they cover over 80,000 ha (200,000 acres) and include habitats of all types, from woods and meadows to mountains and moorlands, and from ponds and rivers to cliffs and beaches. Many are provided with information centres, leaflets and signs. Most of these nature reserves are open to the public.

The Wildlife Trusts also promote wildlife-friendly gardening.

The Royal Horticultural Society (RHS)
The Royal Horticultural Society has teamed up with the Wildlife Trusts to highlight the importance of British gardens for biodiversity with the Wild About Gardens campaign. This aims to bring the worlds of gardening and nature conservation closer together, to increase understanding of the significance of local

wildlife, to celebrate what gardeners are already doing to support wildlife, and to build on existing research into the wildlife potential of domestic gardens.

www.wildaboutgardens.org
www.rhs.org.uk/learning/research/biodiversity

The Royal Society for the Protection of Birds (RSPB)
The Lodge
Sandy
Bedfordshire
SG19 2DL
Tel. 01767 680551
www.rspb.org.uk

The Royal Society for the Protection of Birds is Europe's largest wildlife conservation charity, supported by over 1 million members and with over 160 nature reserves, covering in total more than 275,000 ha (680,000 acres). It has a useful website section devoted to garden wildlife:
www.rspb.org.uk/gardens/guide

BBC
Here is another useful reference:
www.bbc.co.uk/nature/animals/wildbritain/gardenwildlife

Buglife
www.buglife.org.uk

Buglife – the Invertebrate Conservation Trust – is the first organisation in Europe devoted to the conservation of all invertebrates, and is actively engaged in saving Britain's rarest bugs, slugs, snails, bees, wasps, ants, spiders, beetles and many more fascinating invertebrates. It also provides some hints about how to make your garden more attractive to invertebrates.

Further Reading

Sharon Amos
Create a Wildlife Friendly Garden
Collins & Brown, 2005

John Burton and David Tipling
Attracting Wildlife to your Garden
New Holland, 2006

Michael Chinery
Attracting Wildlife to Your Garden
Collins, 2004

Michael Chinery
The Wildlife-Friendly Garden
Harper Collins, 2006

Michael Chinery
Collins Gem Guide: Garden Wildlife
Harper Collins, 2006

Mark Golley
The Complete Garden Wildlife Book
New Holland, 2006

Nicholas Hammond (ed.)
The Wildlife Trust Handbook of Garden Wildlife
New Holland, 2002

Malcolm Tait (ed.)
Wildlife Gardening for Everyone
Think Publishing, 2006

Roy Vickery
The Wildlife Garden at the Natural History Museum
Natural History Museum, 2004

Martin Walters
Gardens for Birds
Aura Books, 2006

Index

Numbers in italics refer to pictures